Bicycle Track Racing

From the Editors of
Bike World Magazine

WORLD PUBLICATIONS
P.O. BOX 366
MOUNTAIN VIEW, CA. 94040

COVER DESIGN BY MARK S. COWANS

Contents

Foreword

Although the majority of American racing cyclists today consider themselves road racers, American cycling's ancestral lineage is in track racing. For the United States was, at the turn of the century, a mecca for international track racing. In fact, bike racing in this country at the turn of the century *was* track racing.

Interest in track cycling waned after that and the drought lasted through the early '60s. Still, the US track racing thread to those previous glory days held firm. It's interesting to note that the recent US international successes in cycling have occurred almost exclusively on the banked ovals. There was the success of the 1955 Pan-American Games 4000-meter pursuit team, Jack Simes ride for a silver medal in the 1000m time trial at the '67 World Championships, the international successes in the '70s of sprinters Steve Woznick, Gibbie Hatton, Tim Mountford, Roger and Sheila Young, Sue Novara, and the gold-medal performance of the US pursuit team in the '75 Pan-American Games.

The track racing heritage in US cycling has been passed down from cyclist to cyclist more by deed and word of mouth than by any sophisticated national coaching scheme or the written word. No national training institute for track cycling exists in the US. No US Cycling Federation manual of track racing has ever been published. There is a void in training literature for track cycling in this country.

Bicycle Track Racing steps into this void. It is not a "bike boom" exploitation book, of which there are many, nor is it over-generalized "fluff" put together by pseudo-experts. *Bicycle Track Racing* is a collection of articles by riders and coaches who have been involved with track racing in all capacities, on a national and international level.

It will be our intention in this book to explain what track racing is all about—how it has developed, how it contrasts with road racing, the different types of events, its significance in US and world cycling, how to get started, what equipment to use, how to train, and much more. We hope that the information presented here will not only help you, the reader, but will also preserve and enhance US involvement and eminence in the sport of track cycling.

At this point we'd like to take the opportunity to thank all the people who contributed to this book, whether with typewriter or camera. A special thanks must go to John Wilcockson, who was the chief contributor, and Jim McCoy, who was of immeasurable help to us as technical editor.

ONE

Fastest and Most Exciting

by John Wilcockson

An active cyclist since childhood, 33-year-old John Wilcockson is experienced in all aspects of cycling, as a tourist, racer and commuter, and has been writing about the sport for almost 15 years. He is the international editor of Bike World *magazine and the former editor of* International Cycle Sport *and* Sports Trader.

Of the various forms of bicycle racing, the fastest and most exciting is track racing. The steeply banked velodromes, the ultra-light track bikes and the competitors themselves are all built for speed. And with the action taking place entirely within sight, spectators can fully appreciate the skills and thrills of this demanding sport.

For a bike rider, a cheering crowd can provide the inspiration for an unexpected level of performance, and the concentrated effort demanded in short races can give full rein to the racer's competitive instincts. Track racing is thus an end in itself as well as being an excellent training ground for those more interested in road competition.

In recent years, American cyclists have won gold medals in track events at the World Championships and the Pan-American Games (the women in the former, men in the latter). This success is due to a renewed interest in the sport, improved coaching methods and a steady increase in the number of actual tracks in existence.

There are definite signs that this expansion will continue into the future, recalling the golden age of the sport in the late 19th and early 20th centuries, when every American city had at least one track and a profusion of track cycling clubs. Professional, as well as amateur, cycle racing was both successful and popular. Americans were regular winners of world titles during the 20-year period from the first World Championships in 1893 to the outbreak of World War I. The sprint and motor-paced events were the specialties of the Americans.

At the same time, the original counterpart of modern six-day racing had its origins in the United States, and the six-day was a permanent feature of the American sports scene through the 1920s and '30s. Since then, track racing rapidly declined in the United States until the slow revival began to gain momentum in the late '60s.

In contrast, the sport has followed a less extreme course in the bastion of bike racing—Europe. Although track racing suffered there in comparison with road racing, there has been a continuity following through from that early golden era. Established events take place throughout the summer months from Easter to the fall, and the winter six-day circuit indoors runs from September to March.

To the uninitiated, all this talk of different types of events and tracks will be confusing, so here is a brief explanation of the basic facts.

By definition, a track is any hard-surfaced circuit that has a regular geometric shape (generally an oval) and is reserved for the purpose of bike racing. There are no permanent indoor tracks in the US. The most common form of track here is exposed to the elements, with concrete or asphalt the usual paving material. These tracks are mostly large (longer than 400 meters), so little banking is required on the turns.

In contrast, a world-class facility, such as the Olympic velodrome at Montreal, is likely to have a circumference of

333m or less. It will consequently have bankings as steep as 50 degrees to the horizontal, permitting safe speeds of up to 50 m.p.h.

The smallest indoor tracks are as short as 150m around, their size being determined by the dimensions of the stadium or hall in which they are erected. Such tracks will normally be prefabricated, with a system of timber trusses supporting a track constructed of hardwood slats running in the direction of travel. Such tracks lead to spectacular and often dangerous racing speeds — the spectacle being accentuated by the steep angle taken by the riders to negotiate the turns and by the rattle of the boards beneath the bikes.

Most indoor tracks are constructed of boards. So are all the fastest outdoor velodromes, such as those at Mexico City, Munich and Rome. Tracks with concrete and asphalt surfaces are slower because of their greater "rolling resistance." However, these tracks are less expensive to build and are also more weather resistant than wooden ones. It is not possible to use unbanked tracks for regular track racing, but grass tracks can be used for racing, although lower gears and heavier tires are required.

The list of events which constitute track racing is virtually endless, but the principal ones that will be encountered are as follows (*denotes event contested in the World Championships):

*Sprint** — Normally 1000m long and contested by two or three riders. Positional sense and timing are as important as speed in the final burst to the line. Only times for the last 200m are officially recorded.

*Tandem sprint** — Same basic format as the one used in the individual sprint, except that the total distance is normally 2000m. Also, the heavier weight of the tandem bicycle alters tactics, with an earlier build-up to top speed required.

*Kilometer time trial** — From a standing start, each competitor rides entirely alone on the track, aiming to complete the 1000m in the shortest time possible.

*Individual pursuit** — Two riders start at directly opposite

Riders whirl around an indoor board track during a six-day (Madison) race in Europe. Six-day racing was very popular in the US before World War II.

stations on the track, the winner being the one who catches his opponent or records the faster time for the complete race. Distances are 5000m for professionals, 4000m for senior men and 3000m for women and junior men.

Team pursuit* — Same format as the individual pursuit, but contested by two teams of four men each. Teams ride in single file, with team members taking turns setting the pace at the front. The time of the third man across the finish line decides the result. The distance is 4000m.

Mass-start — Normally a regular race of 10 miles or 20 kilometers, in which normal road racing techniques and tactics are used.

Points race — A variation on the massed-start, in which the winner is the one who totals the most points in sprints. The sprints are normally contested every fifth lap — depending on the size of track.

Elimination (also known as miss-and-out or devil-take-the-hindmost) — Again, a mass start is used, but the last man over the line each lap has to drop out, until just three riders remain to contest the final sprint for places.

Motor-pacing* — A specialized event with a long history, it is usually contested by six riders, who ride specially constructed bikes with small front wheels. The smaller wheels enable the competitors to ride closer to the large motorcycle pacing machines. Motor-paced races are normally 50 kms long or one hour in duration.

Derny-pacing — A variation on motor-paced racing, but normal track bikes are used and the pacing machine is less powerful.

Madison — A race for teams of two riders in which only one team member competes in the race at any given time (while his partner circles the track slowly). Riders relay each other into the race at regular intervals by means of a Madison change, which is executed by one man pushing his teammate forward while they are alongside each other. Results depend on the number of laps covered by each team during the race and on the number of points won in the intermediate lap sprints.

Handicap — An event in which individual riders start at different points around the track. Handicaps are based on previous form of each rider, with the fastest rider starting at the back. Typical race distance would be one mile, with the first rider across the line the winner.

Omnium — A series of individual races in which points are awarded for the placings in each event. All competitors participate in all events, with the winner being the one who totals the greatest number of points.

Many other types of races are regularly contested, as well as variations on those listed. A novice rider should try as many of the track events as possible to find the one(s) he enjoys most. A road racer would probably have more success at mass-start, pursuit and Madison racing.

The biggest single difference a road rider will experience

when he first races on the track is the track bike, which has no brakes, freewheel or derailleur gears. He will find the bike more responsive to his every movement, and the lack of brakes will help improve his reflexes and bike handling ability when riding in a pack.

The frame of a track bike generally has steeper angles, tighter clearances and less rake than a road machine. The ends of the rear fork open to the rear instead of forward. This eliminates the danger of a rear wheel pulling over. Another safety feature is a lock-ring on the single, fixed sprocket. The ring prevents the sprocket from unscrewing if the rider pedals backwards to slow down.

A typical choice of gear would be 51 x 15 (92 inches) for a first-class track, and 51 x 16 (86 inches) for a track with a rough or bumpy surface. On outdoor tracks, affected by wind, the lower gear would again be used. These gears may sound low to roadmen used to their 53 x 13 top gears, but remember you can't change gear on a track bike. There are no long downhills and the same gear has to be used for riding into and with the wind in quick succession. Most importantly, the gear must be low enough to enable you to accelerate from a possible standstill − in a match sprint, for instance − to top speed in the shortest possible time.

Complete mechanical efficiency is essential, of course, but the wheels and tires are probably the most important items on a track bike. Rigidity and lightness are the key factors here.

Rigidity is obtained by using large flange hubs (*not* quick-release) and spokes that are tied-and-soldered. Sprinters, who put more stress on a wheel, will use 36 spokes (or even 40 on a very steeply banked track where high centrifugal forces are developed). Pursuiters, on the other hand, use 28 spokes, or even 24 on the best tracks.

For lightness, a narrower section rim and tire are used, the rim being of a wood-insert type and the tubular fabric probably being silk. The tire has a smooth tread and always weighs less than 200 grams. Some track bike tires weigh as little as 100 grams.

Shellac is used instead of rubber solution to stick the tubulars to the rim. Shellac provides a firmer bond, eliminating any chance of a tire rolling off. In motor-paced racing, it is even common to wrap tire and rim with tape at a number of points around the wheel.

Other features of a track bike which separate it from a road bike are less bulky pedals, a higher bottom bracket and (for rigidity) a steel stem and handlebars. The drop of the handlebars will probably be greater on a track bike — especially for sprinting, where an exaggerated forward or power position can be used for the shorter time intervals of maximum effort.

MAIN TRACK RACING AREAS

Now you know what sort of bike to use and the various events which are contested on the track. But where will you race?

Details on where tracks are located throughout North America are included in the appendix. But the main US track racing areas (where most of the national champions come from as well) are southern California (the Encino track being the site of competition), northern California (the San Jose track), the Midwest (where the Northbrook, Ill., track is frequently used for the National Championships) and the East (with tracks in New York, New Jersey and Pennsylvania).

In Canada, British Columbia and Ontario currently produce the top riders. The new Olympic track in Montreal should also encourage cyclists from Quebec to reach top class.

The competition schedule at the various tracks usually consists of weekly club-sponsored meets throughout the summer, with an occasional open meet, when riders from other areas also take part. Some tracks also organize special coaching sessions for young people to introduce them to the sport.

The main stumbling block to raising the standards in track racing on this continent is the physical impossibility of regular competition between riders from all over the country (this is true for both Canada and the United States). In fact, the only time riders get the chance to pit themselves against those from other areas is in the annual national championships.

In contrast, track riders in European countries have ample opportunity to compete against all their main rivals, both at home and abroad. In Britain, for example, there are about a dozen mid-week track leagues at the major tracks, as well as open meets every weekend. With travel distances so much shorter than in North America, a keen rider will compete at most of the open promotions. In addition, there are frequent international meets, featuring matches against national teams from overseas.

Both amateur and professional track racing in Europe is probably as strong today as it has been at any time since the Second World War. There is regular open competition between professionals and amateurs, including the major Grand Prix sprint meets at such places as Paris, Moscow, Copenhagen and Milan.

Winter racing is also extremely successful at the indoor velodromes in Belgium, Holland, East Germany, West Germany and Switzerland. And six-day races are promoted in England, France, Denmark, Italy, Belgium, Germany, Holland and Switzerland.

Perhaps the crowds at top meets today still do not match those at meets in the 1920s and '30s, but performances at the Olympics and the World Championships show that track riders are faster and fitter today than at any other period in history. The sport is also expanding in the rest of the world, with competitors from South America, the Caribbean, Australia and Japan proving the most successful in international competition.

Track cycling is also popular in South Africa, but the most surprising outpost of the sport is Japan. There, hundreds of professional racing cyclists compete in meets which draw thousands of spectators. These are most unusual meets, more akin to dog racing than bike racing. Each race is fairly short. A mass start is used, the riders starting from special starting gates. The reason for the big crowds is that this is one of the few forms of legal gambling in Japan. The "sport" is so successful that many of the top men earn huge salaries and the official

World-class British pursuiter Ian Hallam (right) shows his versatility by winning a sprint race over British sprint champion Ernie Crutchlow.

promoting body maintains its own opulent coaching center, where prospective track riders undergo intensive training to groom them for racing careers.

GLAMOR AND DRAMA

Top class bike track meets are full of glamor and drama. There is a wonderful aesthetic interplay between the smooth surface of the track, the bright colors of silk jerseys and the glinting flashes of sunshine, or lights, on sparkling spokes. The spectators are loud and enthusiastic, cheering their favorites and shouting catcalls at the bad guys who win by using dangerous tactics.

The sense of drama and tension is perhaps best captured in match sprinting, the classic of all track events. Man against man; match sprinting is a battle of wits as much as a test of strength and speed. There is a slow but absorbing build-up from the moment the starter holds the starting pistol aloft and fires.

The rider on the inside has to move off in front and rides slowly round the track, perhaps taking a line at the top of the banking to see if his opponent's nerves are strong enough for him to balance at a slow speed on a 50-degree slope. After a lap, the man at the front is not obliged to retain the lead, according to *Union Cycliste Internationale* rules. This is where the climax of the tactical battle can occur.

The front rider may come to a standstill, balancing his bike in place in an attempt to make his opponent take the lead. (It is usually best to be behind your opponent when the sprint starts, because you can see exactly what he is doing *and* you can make a surprise jump before he can react.) During the standstill both riders will watch each other for the slightest movement or loss of balance. The referee will also be looking intently, pistol ready in case either rider makes a backward movement. If that happens there would be a restart, with the rider who was at fault taking the front position.

Between two experienced competitors, a standstill can have the dramatic quality of a Hitchcock thriller: the crowd is silent, absorbed by the psychological parrying, waiting for the first pedal thrust. Perhaps it will be a killing move, if one sprinter jumps while the other has a momentary cramp or has positioned his front wheel at too sharp an angle up the banking. Or perhaps the first competitor to move will only pedal ahead slowly, watching what his opponent is doing.

If the latter happens, the final phase of action will now start. The speed will slowly increase, with the game of cat-and-mouse being played up and down the banking, one rider following the other. Race fans will be speculating on the final moves — a quick dive from the top of the banking by the leader? Or a dramatic dive on the inside by the man at the back?

A shout of expectation will swell from the stands, as the two sprinters are suddenly racing flat out. This is the part of the race when anything can happen — a swerve by the leader that could lead to disqualification, or maybe a clash of wheels or elbows that could result in a spectacular spill. Yes, match sprinting is a race which can take many different turns in a short space of time. And at the end some races are so close that the winner isn't known until the finish photos are studied.

When you also consider that each sprint match is the best of three runs, and that one rider could have as many as six races in an evening, you will see that even a sprinter must have both mental and physical stamina in addition to the obvious requirements of speed and strength.

For the spectators, the sprint will be just one highlight among many during a meet. At World and National Championships, tension reaches a peak on the last night when the finals in the various events are contested. This is when months of preparation and training all come together in the ultimate test of competition. Nerves play a major part in any rider's performance, and many a title has been lost through an inexperienced performer losing his confidence at a time when he needed it most.

What makes a champion? Natural talent, certainly, but basically it is a combination of many qualities. Any track rider must first be strong enough to undertake the necessary training. Next comes the dedication to continually practice his specialty, whether that specialty is a rapid start in the case of a kilometer man or a fast finish in the case of a sprinter. Intelligence is also high on the list — the brains to outwit an opponent and to learn from previous errors. And then there is confidence, to enable a competitor to carry plans through as well as to channel energy into fruitful efforts rather than dissipating it in "impossible" attacks.

A different combination of qualities and skills is needed for each event — but the requirements are not so different that you have to concentrate entirely on a single discipline. There are innumerable instances of cyclists who have been successful at many facets of the sport.

One of the leading track professionals today is the Belgian ace Patrick Sercu, who is a top rider in the winter season of six-day racing, as well as being a former Olympic kilometer champion and ex-world sprint champion. In addition, Sercu has been immensely successful in road racing, with numerous stage victories in the Tour de France and Giro d'Italia to his credit.

Another example, in the amateur ranks, is the English rider Ian Hallam. He is best known as a pursuiter (with Olympic and World Championship medals), but he has also won national titles at the kilometer time trial. He is also one of his country's leading 25-mile time trialists on the road and is a frequent road race winner, with stage wins in tough races like the Tour of Britain.

One of the most versatile characters in the history of track racing was the stocky Australian Sid Patterson, who went to Europe in 1949 and surprisingly won the world amateur sprint title. In the following year's World Championships he won the 4000-meter pursuit. He later went on to claim two more pursuit championships as a professional. He is the only man to have performed this "impossible" double — victory in the sprint and pursuit — in world-class competition.

The greatest names of the past, however, have been the specialists — men like the incomparable Belgian sprinter Jef Scherens, who won the world professional sprint championship six times in succession (1932-'37). He came back after the Second World War to notch his seventh title in 1947, a decade later. Not only was Scherens successful, but he was a showman, with the ability to judge every sprint to the last millimeter —

invariably winning his races by waiting until the final straight to make his effort from behind. His skill was particularly surprising considering he was much shorter and lighter than the average sprinter (sprinters are generally large-framed).

There had been a great tradition of sprint champions before Scherens, such as the big Dutchman Toni Moeskops, who won five pro titles between 1921 and 1926, and the Dane Ellegaard, six-time professional champion between 1901 and 1911. Of the amateurs, perhaps the greatest sprinter in the early part of the century was the handsome, well-built Englishman Bill Bailey, winner of the world title in 1909, 1910, 1911 and 1913.

During this period, American track cyclists experienced their greatest success with amateur titles going to Hurley (1904) and McDougall (1912), and professional championships to Lawson (1904) and Kramer (1912). Other Americans who notched World Championship victories in the sprint were Zimmerman (1893), Banker (1898) and Taylor (1899).

Since World War II, professional sprinting has enjoyed varied popularity. It achieved its most successful period in the years leading up to the mid-'50s, when the crowds flocked to see the season-long battles across Europe between such riders as the Dutch stars Arie Van Vliet and Jan Derksen, the British master Reg Harris, the ebullient Swiss showman Oscar Plattner, Italy's instinctive sprinter Antonio Maspes and the roly-poly Frenchman Michel Rousseau.

All of these men were capable of winning the world championship and all of them did, so the four title victories by Harris between 1949 and 1954 have added significance. The English star was completely self-motivated, and owed much of his success to his tremendously tough training routine. He had an enormous public following, which was emphasized by the support he received when he made a surprise comeback in 1974 to win the British sprint championship. He was in his 50s at the time.

After Harris, the professional sprint title became the near-personal property of the Italian Maspes, who was champion seven times between 1955 and 1964. Since then, no rider has dominated professional sprinting. Perhaps the reason is that the top sprinter in the world today, Daniel Morelon of France, six-time amateur world champion and twice Olympic champion, refuses to turn professional. He says he would not be able to make a reasonable living as a purely professional sprinter.

Like sprinting, motor-paced racing has a long history, but this event, too, has been in decline over the past decade. The last great name in professional motor-paced racing was the little Spaniard Timoner, winner of the world title six times between 1955 and 1965.

One reason for the recent eclipse of this potentially spectacular event was the introduction of derny-paced racing to the winter velodromes. The most outstanding performers behind these little motors were the extraordinary Dutchman Peter Post (world record holder for the number of six-day victories) and the superb Belgian pace follower Theo Verschueren, who, in fact, adapted his style to the big motors to win the world title in 1971.

This branch of track racing was far more competitive and popular earlier in this century, and was an essential part of any worthwhile track meet. Due to the stiff competition, few men could dominate affairs — unlike the case in sprinting. But motor-paced racing also developed a rather bad reputation for "fixing" of race results by the trainers (the men riding the pacing motors), who were not averse to taking bribes.

The most successful champions in motor-paced racing during this era were the Belgian rider Victor Linart (professional champion in 1921, '24, '26 and '27) and the remarkable British performer Leon Meredith (amateur champion seven times between 1904 and 1913).

Pursuit racing was not introduced to the World Championships until after World War II, but in the 30 years since then some remarkable riders have placed their names in the record books. Fausto Coppi, probably the greatest roadman of all time, won the professional world title in 1947 and '49. The brilliant Frenchman Roger Riviere won three pro titles ('57, '58 and '59) and, like Coppi, was a long-time holder of the one-hour world

A dramatic shot of US match sprinters Steve Woznick (right) and Carl Leusenkamp flying through a turn at full speed. Woznick won the sprint gold medal in the 1975 Pan-American Games, Leusenkamp took the bronze.

Robert George

record (both men set their records on Milan's Vigorelli board track). And the outstanding West German Rudi Altig followed up his amateur title victory in 1959 with two professional rainbow jerseys (awarded to world champions) in the succeeding two years.

The most prolific winners of the professional title have been the Italians Guido Messina ('54, '55 and '56) and Leandro Faggan ('63, '65 and '66), and the tall, stylish Englishman Hugh Porter (who won four titles between 1968 and '73). Current champion is Holland's Roy Schuiten, whose victory in the 1974 championships took place just a few weeks after he left the amateur ranks.

Amateur pursuiting is even more competitive than the professional version. As a result, few riders have been able to win the amateur title more than once. The only ones to do so have been Messina ('48 and '53), Englishman Norman Sheil ('55 and '58), Tiemen Groen of the Netherlands (who scored a hat-trick by winning in '64, '65 and '66) and the Swiss racer Xaver Kurmann ('69 and '70).

Finally, this brief review of the track scene would not be complete without a mention of women's racing. Women's events weren't included in the World Championships until 1958. At present the only track events for women in the championships are the sprint and pursuit. The sprint was completely monopolized by the Russians – with the remarkable Galina Ermolaeva winning five titles—until the breakthrough by US star Sheila Young, who won the world title in 1974. Sheila's victory was followed by that of another American, Sue Novara, who won in 1975.

As for pursuiting, the Russian women have met much stiffer opposition. The most successful champion has been Britain's Beryl Burton, who won five titles between 1959 and '66. Mrs. Burton's greatest rival was the powerful Belgian Yvonne Reynders (who won the championship in '61, '64 and '65), while her successor was the little locomotive from the USSR, Tamara Garkushina.

From this introduction you'll have learned that track racing has great variety and a long history. In the following chapters, many of the different aspects of track racing will be examined in greater depth. The emphasis will be on guiding the track newcomer along the right course towards a successful career.

United States racing cyclists have a better opportunity today to compete and improve than at any time in 50 years. Besides regular meets at the tracks listed in this book, there are annual area and state championships and the National Championships.

These events are run by the United States Cycling Federation (USCF), the body that also selects and sends teams to the annual World Championships (for senior men, women and juniors) and (in conjunction with the US Olympic Committee) to the Olympics and Pan-American Games.

In Canada, the governing body is the Canadian Cycling Association.

TWO

Getting Started

by William Sanders

William Sanders of Little Rock, Ark., is a long-time contributor to Bike World *magazine. He currently writes the* Bike World *column "At the Starting Line," which is aimed at the novice racer. He has been involved in all phases of bike racing and actively participates in races.*

Track racing is a bargain. While some special equipment is needed, the expense involved is quite a bit less than that associated with road racing.

If you have already done some road racing or have worn road-race outfits for touring, you've already got the basic clothing. Any helmet which meets United States Cycling Federation standards is good enough for the track. So is any quality racing shoe with solidly mounted cleats, though specialized track footgear does exist. Regulation black shorts are standard also. ("Madison" shorts are made for certain track events. These shorts are designed to give your partner a grip in throwing you into the fray. But you probably won't be doing that sort of racing for quite some time.)

A slick-finished track jersey should be worn whenever possible. Many riders wear two of these, as the sliding effect reduces abrasions in a crash. This might be a good idea for a novice.

The only special equipment you've got to have is the track bike, and even this is dirt cheap by modern price standards. Even the high quality models, such as the track version of the Schwinn Paramount, cost about a third less than the equivalent road model — a saving of perhaps $200 or more. This is partly because you're not paying for brakes, derailleurs, freewheel, etc. Also, the dealer tends to be very helpful and considerate about track bikes, because he's got a much smaller market for them. This last point also affects the used track bike situation; the great sleepers of the bike world are the nearly new track bikes offered for sale by people who had to move to an area with no track, or simply decided track "wasn't their bag." (But check those bearings. Track riders, for some reason I've never understood, tend to be terribly rough on hubs.)

There are inexpensive track bikes designed for beginners. These are heavier and less beautifully finished than the Schwinn or Raleigh offerings — let alone the gorgeous Continental jobs like Guerciotti — but a basic bike is not nearly the handicap on the track that it might be on the road. After all, there are no hills to climb, so weight matters less. Also, the lack of complex components, such as derailleurs, eliminates a common source of trouble from "cheapo" equipment.

This inexpensive type of bike, with straight-gauge frame, cottered steel crank and rather unsophisticated wheels, may have no status, but it will do perfectly well for the beginner to master the techniques of track riding. It should see him or her through a season of novice competition. (Track riders, in any case, are far less snobbish about equipment than roadmen.)

Gitane sells a very reliable track bike at quite a low price — less than $200 the last time I checked. And I have seen a Urago, apparently an entirely adequate bike, sold for even less.

A person who has the money could get a track Paramount. Another good bike is the Raleigh, as sold over the counter, with a selection of cogs. But it would be very foolish, even if you were rich, to buy a custom track frame at the outset. There are several specialties in this sport, and a pursuit frame, for example, is very different from a sprint frame. The novice could not know what his or her specialty is going to be without trying almost all the events.

With track bikes being so inexpensive, there is little point in trying to convert a road bike unless one is really short of money. One problem area in converting a road bike would be the wheels. You would need a pair of track wheels, or else you'd have to get a pair of track hubs and lace up your own. But track wheels are a whole new world of stresses and strains, and very few people can build track wheels well. And contrary to some widely disseminated information which appeared in a leading racing magazine, you *cannot* screw track cogs onto a road hub.

(It is not a matter of merely screwing a single cog onto a road hub. A track cog by itself could be screwed onto a BSA ["English"] threaded road hub, but not onto the French threaded type. Also, the locking ring will *not* go on the road hub, and this ring is a vital part of the fixed-gear power train; while some track riders do not use the locking ring, the practice is very unwise and most officials will not allow it if they spot it. Without the locking ring, you don't have the same control over the bike – a dangerous business.

Track hubs also use nuts rather than quick-release levers; the latter are illegal in mass-start track events. And finally, track wheels need to be built to a different set of specifications than road wheels, because the stresses are entirely different and the cornering forces are tremendous.)

If you had a pair of track wheels you could, theoretically, strip your road bike down – removing brakes, derailleurs, and wheels – and create something technically legal. But you still would not have a track bike. In order to keep from hanging pedals on the banking and crashing, you need shorter crank arms – 165mm – which would be another expense. Then you'd want different chainrings and a chain...but by now you'd have spent almost enough to buy a used track bike of the simpler sort. I've seen a secondhand Gitane beginner model sold for under $100, and they're a lot more bike than any reworked road machine.

Not sure you want to get involved with track racing to that extent? May I point out, then, that even if you quit the track, a track bike is an excellent machine for early season training for the road. If fitted with a front-wheel brake and heavier tires, it makes a neat bike for scooting around town (and the thieves will leave it alone because it obviously isn't a "10-speed"!).

INITIAL TRAINING

You will learn how to train for competition in the next chapter, but before you can go far you will have to spend a little time learning the basic skills of operating a track bike in its natural habitat, the velodrome. (If you have to ride on a flat, unbanked course because there's no track in your area, my heart goes out to you. There are no solutions to your problems, short of moving or having a lot of relatives on the city council who can get a velodrome built.)

For your first few sessions the bike should be fitted with a fairly low gear, in the lower to mid-60s. Learning to ride on the track will require enough work without the distraction of trying to turn a "gorilla" gear. Also, you will want to begin by riding slowly, and this is easier in a lower gear.

Begin by riding at low speed around the inner perimeter of the track. Experiment with the fixed gear. It isn't as hard to operate as you might think. Work on controlling your speed by means of backpedaling. Be cautious at first; don't go practicing your sudden stops if there are people behind you. Try to get comfortable on the bike, and become confident in your bike handling ability.

Now you can try going up higher on the track and take the banking at speed. No matter how hard it is, rid yourself of the notion that you're going to fall off or slide down the banking. As long as you're moving at any sort of respectable speed, you aren't going to fall off. This is not the "wall of death" circus stunt it might appear. Besides, very few American velodromes are steeply banked anyway. It is easier and safer to learn to ride

A coach is almost a necessity to a track rider. The place to find good coaching is at a track like this. Shown here is the Trexlertown (Penn.) velodrome on the day it opened.

the banking than to master fast cornering on a criterium or road course.

It will be best if you can do your early training with someone (a friend or coach) who has had some sort of track experience. Ideally, you would have the track to yourselves. But if you have to do your early riding with a lot of people on the track, remember to be considerate. Don't go swinging suddenly up or down without checking behind, and always ride a straight line. Stay alert; things happen fast on the tracks, even in practice, and there isn't a lot of room to maneuver. Many track managements will summarily throw a reckless rider off the track, as is only right.

In slow-speed practice, ride down close to the inner edge of the track — the "pole line." Get up high, near the fence, when trying high-speed techniques.

Riding in the middle is dangerous for you and others. There

will be people, particularly pace groups, moving much faster than you. And if you're in the middle, they will have no way of knowing what you're about to do, or on which side to pass.

CLUBS AND COACHES

Loners have it rough on the track; a coach is almost a requirement for any real success. Even a little informal coaching by another rider will be better than trying to figure it all out by yourself. Those who for some reason cannot take advice or criticism will have a hard time of it in track racing.

Great track stars are almost invariably thought of and talked about in connection with their coaches. There is even the implication that the coach and rider operate as a team, such as world amateur sprint champion Daniel Morelon and his coach Toto Gerardin.

While the road coach must follow riders around on a motorcycle or in a car and has trouble seeing what is going on at times, the track coach is right there in the infield and can observe at close range every detail of the rider's position, technique, tactics and so on. Track riders are in sight, in Ralph Hurne's words, like "prunes on a plate." This gives the coach the opportunity to correct the most minute problems, and when the coach speaks, a wise rider listens.

This is not to say you must slavishly accept everything your coach tells you and never think at all for yourself. The greatest coach can be mistaken at times. As the Japanese say, "Even monkeys sometimes fall out of trees." But until you have had enough racing experience to form qualified opinions, it would be better to go along with the coach's suggestions, even though some of the ideas might seem odd at first.

Trying to train by yourself is an absolute last resort. If there is no coach, at least try to get in some riding in groups. Otherwise, you will never learn the complex art of maneuvering in a big bunch, trading pace in team events, or the rodeo tricks of match sprinting. Even to ride the kilo or pursuit, you need at least a helper in the infield with a stopwatch.

Fortunately, it is relatively easy to find a coach and a

club because the two generally go together in the track world. Just by hanging around a track and watching, you should be able to see how harmoniously the various teams work together, whether they have a good relationship with their coaches, and perhaps get an idea which club in your area would best suit your needs and disposition.

Generally speaking, where there are velodromes, there are good clubs and coaches.

If you are lucky, you may even get a chance to get in on one of the workshops sometimes conducted at the major tracks by international-level coaches.

THE QUESTION OF AGE

The youngest age to begin track racing is fixed by the USCF rule book at eight, or, since this refers to age at the first of the year, usually nine. But should one begin racing at such a young age? This is not an easy question to answer.

Not only do children differ in maturity; so do parents. Unfortunately, the infamous "Little League mentality" is not unknown in bike racing, and it tends to find its worst outlets at the track. Parents often display the most incredible and obnoxious behavior, screaming abuse at their child should he get dropped. In addition to discrediting the sport in the eyes of spectators, these people will probably see to it that their child is totally turned off with bike racing by age 11.

Many psychologists argue that children this age are not well served by placing them in such a demanding sport, where their time and attention is unnaturally focused at an age when they should be interested in a wide spectrum of activities and sports.

Be that as it may, whatever age the young rider does begin, the track has certain advantages. Supervision is more complete than on the road, and the track is generally safer, being free of cars, trucks, large dogs and so on. Track crashes tend to be mostly skin-scrapers rather than hospital cases. There are no hillclimbs to strain young hearts or downhills to build up dangerous speeds.

Finally — and I think this is the most important point of all

— beginning on the track builds better pedaling and bike handling skills, quicker reflexes and cooler nerves. This develops a more complete cyclist, even if he or she later forsakes the track for the road.

What about the older rider?

The senior cyclist has even more reason to ride the track. Certainly age should be no barrier, given decent physical condition. Since there are no hills to climb and the events are of shorter duration, the veteran may find track racing less physically taxing. The USCF doesn't even have a Veterans class in track at championship level, because the best Veteran-age cyclists do not seem to feel any handicap competing against younger riders. Jack Disney is still one of the top sprinters in the country and regularly defeats boys half his age. Disney is, of course, exceptional for any age group, but there is no reason why the principle should not apply at all levels.

WOMEN

There is one more group with a special interest in track: female competitors. Many feel resentful at not being taken seriously by officials or male riders. There is no doubt that this is often true on the road — too often — but in track, thanks largely to the truly outstanding accomplishments of sprinters Sheila Young and Sue Novara and pursuiter Miji Reoch, women are regarded with respect. In fact, they sometimes upstage the men. This should be something of a refreshing change to female cyclists who have been treated as some sort of side-show. But be warned! The competition in this class is really ferocious. Be ready to do some hard riding if you want to get up there with people like Novara, Young and Reoch.

TRACK RACING FOR THE ROAD RIDER

Should the road racer get involved in track?

A lot depends on the type of rider. Track racers vary a lot in physical type — Steve Woznick is about twice as big as Roger Young. But in general the track racer tends to be a powerful, "nervous," rather aggressive type.

A road racer who does well at short criteriums will probably be good at mass-start track events. A roadman noted for a strong sprint might be a good track sprinter as well, and those with a particularly long sprint could do well at the kilo. Almost any strong road rider will be good at the pursuit. An example is Mike Neel, who is otherwise not much associated with the track.

On the other hand, the smaller, birdlike climber isn't likely to do well on the track. George Mount would be a rather improbable figure in a kilo or sprint, for example — just as Steve Woznick would never be able to follow George up a steep mountain road.

A rider who has not been doing well in road racing for various reasons, such as lack of patience in long events, inability to climb or a limited time to train for endurance, might find new opportunities on the track. I have seen it happen. People who were about to give up cycling completely would try track as a last resort and suddenly start winning races. In particular, the very heavy rider should check out the track. With no mountains to climb, and a banking to help hold the rider's bulk in a turn, the big, blocky cyclist may find considerable success in track racing, especially the sprint.

What about the road racer who intends to remain primarily on the road? Is there any point to bother with track other than mere variety?

Many experts believe that track experience is helpful to any cyclist: road racer, criterium specialist, time trialist, cyclo-crosser—even the serious tourist, strange as that idea may be. The benefits include:

1) Improved bike handling. Experience in the fast-moving world of the velodrome develops a safer, more agile bike handler.

2) Clean pedal style. The use of a fixed gear in training is a well-known device to improve pedal technique, and is used even on road bikes in early training. The subtle pressures of track-bike pedaling, in which the pedals are used both to speed up and slow down, develop greater sensitivity and a smooth, spinning motion that saves energy and is very fast on any type of bike.

3) Judgment. Moving fast without brakes in a restricted area teaches a rider to think fast and react instantly. This not only can win races but perhaps save the rider's life some day.

4) Confidence. Having ridden in this demanding, exciting sport, you become more confident of your ability to deal with any situation. You will find yourself able to thread calmly through the biggest road packs without flinching. Since track riders have a reputation for being crafty, fast and tough, you will also find yourself more respected among the roadmen. They will be less eager to play cute tricks on you, such as chopping you in criteriums or cutting you off in bunch sprints.

5) Teamwork. A group of riders accustomed to such demanding specialties as the team pursuit can put their precision and cooperation to good use, reducing the less coordinated opposition to virtual helplessness. In this country, team riding is such a rare accomplishment that experience in it gives a rider a big advantage on the road.

6) Recovery. Mass-start track racing involves a great deal of variation in speed and the need for sudden acceleration. Track is, therefore, a fine way to improve one's recovery from sudden effort, and this is useful in making or chasing breaks on the road. This effect is increased by having only one gear — you can't shift up or down to give your legs a break.

7) Night riding. In the case of a modern track with flood-lights and a good program, track gives you a chance to do some night riding. This is a definite plus if your time is limited by work or school.

I might add, by way of clinching all this, that I once ran into a group of top road riders of my acquaintance — names by no stretch of the imagination associated with the banked track — at Northbrook's famous velodrome. "You guys serious?" I asked.

The reaction was very honest. "We know we're gonna get killed," they said. "But even a little of this business does wonders for your road work."

It might do wonders for yours, too.

Setting Up Your Bike

by Vic Black

A 34-year-old mechanical designer, Vic Black served as the northern California area representative for cycling last year, A former racer, he has been vitally involved in cycling organizational work in recent years. He is regarded as one of the best—if not the best—cycling announcers in the US. Vic is a member of the Pedali Alpini cycling club in Menlo Park, Calif.

Body position and the way the bike is set up (e.g., saddle placement) are of key importance to the track rider. Since the physical structure of each rider is different, there can be no hard and fast rules for setting up a track bike. What is offered here is a basic starting point. You will need to experiment, making minor adjustments until your position on the bike is perfectly suited to your body, your riding style and the type of racing you will be doing.

By feeling the forces on your body and analyzing them, you will be able to tell if your bike is properly set up. Don't be afraid to try something a little different. Sometimes a rider will set up an exaggerated, inefficient position and live with it. This demonstrates the remarkable adaptability of the human body.

The trick is to find a position which is aerodynamic, allows for easy breathing, gives a balanced, responsive feel to the bicycle and facilitates pedal action. Your position shouldn't determine your style, but it should provide a relaxed crouch

31

Robert George

Body position and bike set-up for the pursuit. Rider is Jim Mensching, 2nd in '73 US Championships.

allowing excellent control and efficient application of power without a stretched-out or bunched-up feeling.

Good form on a track bike is heavily dependent on saddle placement. Saddle position is almost infinitely variable within its range of adjustments (possible in four directions). Not only may the saddle be raised and lowered or rotated about the seat pin in a horizontal manner, but it may also be moved fore and aft and the tip may be tilted up or down to accommodate various frame angles. As a result of this wide range of adjustments, you will probably need to make several attempts at finding the proper saddle position.

First, make sure the saddle is not rotated. A saddle that is rotated to the right or left will apply pressure to the inside of one thigh and not the other. A rotated saddle is visually obvious. It can be detected by holding the front wheel between your legs and sighting along the top tube to the saddle and back to the rear wheel.

The type of racing you plan to do will determine how far forward the saddle should be placed. During an all-out sprint, the abdominal muscles contract and the torso is pulled forward. Therefore, sprinters usually mount the saddle slightly more forward than pursuiters and middle-distance riders.

For sprinters, the front tip of the saddle should be approximately ½–1½ inches behind the center of the bottom bracket. For pursuiters, the saddle can be moved back 1½ to 2½ inches behind the bottom bracket. You can easily check the saddle position by hanging a weighted string from the saddle tip with the bike standing on a level floor.

Nearly all types of riding require that the saddle be level. Tipping the nose of the saddle up will rotate the pelvis back. Reaching for the handlebars from this position will excessively stretch the long muscles of the lower back. Large forces will also be placed on the lumbar vertebrae in the small of the back.

Tipping the nose of the saddle down will cause you to slip forward, making it difficult to maintain a constant position on the saddle during sprints. Control of the bike is impossible with a constantly shifting position.

The best position is to have the saddle perfectly parallel to the ground. Use a small bubble level to determine if the saddle is in this position. First, check the floor and find a spot that is level. Next, with the bike held in a vertical riding position on that level spot, place a yardstick on the saddle parallel to the top tube. Now place the bubble level on the yardstick over the saddle. This will give you a good indication of whether or not the saddle is level.

Occasionally a rider tips the nose of the saddle down so he can reach the pedals. This is a clear-cut indication that the saddle is too high. Due to the differences in body structure and riding style, some riders will want to tip the saddle slightly up, although for most riders this makes it difficult to spin the cranks at highest speed. The saddle should *never* be tipped down.

Saddle height is somewhat dependent on the type of race you intend to ride. Sprinters use the highest positions while pursuiters and middle-distance riders use a lower position. Road riders use the lowest saddle positions.

As a starting point in determining saddle height, a sprinter should get onto the bike with his feet in the toe clips and the crank at its lowest point. There should be just a slight bend in the knee. This will allow full use of the leg muscles during sprints. Pursuiters should get onto the bike with the crank at its lowest point and with the heel on the pedal. There should be just a slight bend in the knee.

When the saddle is too high, the leg will be over-extended and the toes may even point downward in order to reach the bottom of the crank arc. This will usually cause a stretching sensation in the hamstrings behind the thighs, and a side-to-side hip movement. At no time should the hips move from side to side during pedaling.

Too low a saddle position will cause a bunched-up feeling and the knees may even hit the chest. This will interfere with breathing. Worse yet, it will put tremendous strain on the knees and can damage cartilage in the knee joint.

After determining a good position for your saddle, you will need to adjust your handlebars.

Sprint 'bars are normally made of steel to withstand the powerful forces put on them during jumps and sprints. They are deeply curved and the extensions are dropped down in the front so rider and bike will present a more aerodynamic profile. Sprint handlebars and extensions should be chosen to match your own body structure. The choice will depend on how long your upper torso is, the length of your arms and the suppleness of your spinal column. Make sure your elbows don't interfere with your knees and that you are able to look back to check easily on your opponent.

After arriving at an efficient sprint position using steel sprint 'bars and sloping extension, a new position should be found for pursuits. Pursuit races will be easier to ride in a more relaxed position with the handlebars higher than for sprints. When only one bike is available, the position can be changed by raising the extension. Another alternative is to carry two sets of handlebars and extensions to the track. Forces on the handlebars are not as severe in time trials and pursuits as those encountered during sprints, so steel 'bars are not required. A set of aluminum road 'bars will make breathing easier. They should be chosen to match the width of your shoulders.

Some riders will have one bike for sprints and another for pursuits.

Normally, track frames are somewhat smaller than road frames. A track frame must have a high bottom bracket so that the track may be ridden slowly without the right pedal hitting the banking. A frame made especially for pursuit will have a high bottom bracket but will provide a more spread-out riding position than a sprint bike. Due to the speeds achieved on the track, the handlebars would be too high for aerodynamic efficiency if the track bike frame was as big as the frame on a road bike.

A properly designed bicycle is well balanced. Unmounted, the bike will have about half its weight on each wheel. With a rider in the saddle, the recommended weight distribution, for best handling, is 45 per cent of the weight on the front wheel and 55 per cent on the rear wheel. If your bicycle is set up properly, you should obtain this approximate weight distribution automatically.

You can check weight distribution easily by using a bathroom scale placed on a level floor. Set the front wheel of the bike on the scale. Place the rear wheel on a telephone directory, a stack of books or a block of wood so that both wheels are the same distance above the floor. Carefully mount the bike and assume a riding position with feet in the toe clips and hands on the handlebar hooks. This is easiest to do next to a wall. Place one hip against the wall for balance or have a friend hold you upright.

Read and record the weight shown on the scale.

Now turn the bike around and place the rear wheel on the scale. Repeat the procedure. By adding the two weights together you will have the total weight of rider and bike. Divide the front wheel reading by the total to find what percentage of the weight is on the front wheel. Divide the rear wheel reading by the total to find the rear percentage.

An actual example will illustrate the procedure. A 155-pound rider found that his front wheel supported 77 pounds while his rear wheel supported 97 pounds. The total is 174 pounds. This tells us that his bike weighs 19 pounds (i.e., 174-155=19). The weight on the front divided by the total is 77/174 = 44.2%. The weight on the rear divided by the total is 97/174=55.8%. This is very close to the recommended weight distribution.

THREE

Training For Track Racing

An Interview with Veteran Racer-Coach
Don Peterson, by Jim McCoy

Californian Don Peterson, now 50, started racing as a 16-year-old in 1939 on a San Jose board track. In those days, when a bike racer was given the same respect accorded a football player, he raced in front of standing room only crowds of over 2,500. Although he won several 100 km road races before World War II, his forte has always been the track, where he won the Senior National Championship two-mile in 1941. After suffering a broken back in a track spill in Burbank, Calif., in 1953, Don stayed out of the sport until 1960, when he started cycling again to help his son Terry develop as a racer.

Don did a stint as president of the Northern California Cycling Association in the '60s but felt like he was "spinning his wheels." Since then he has concentrated more on coaching and less on riding, although he still competes and places in Category I criteriums, and in 1974 won the Veterans State Road Championship in northern California.

His general coaching philosophy is to work hard at the local level, developing riders within the San Jose Bicycle Club (of which he is currently president). Evidence of his coaching skill is undeniable, especially in working with junior riders. Recent riders he's coached include Keith Mowen, 1972 Olympian; Bill Tout, Northern California Road and Pursuit Champion, 1971; Junior World Team members Steve Lundgren (Road) and Paul Wilson (Track), 1973; Lundgren and Chris Haley (Road), 1974; Ken Anderson (Road), 1975; National Champions Jim Gentes (Jr. Cyclocross), and Chris Springer (Intermediate Road and Track), 1975.

Don, a track racer is looking for a place to compete, in the pure sense; you have always advocated track racing as good training for the road racer. What type of training for track do you advocate?

Peterson: When we talk about training for track, primarily we're talking about training for a *fast* race. It doesn't matter if that race is a criterium (on the road) or a track race, your training is about the same.

But as far as extensive training *on* the track is concerned, I really don't recommend it. Get used to a track if you are going to specialize—if you are a match sprinter, then it is a required place to train periodically. But in general, when you ride on the track you must run high gears and this is, in my opinion, not the best way to train; I won't set up a small gear on the track. It is difficult to ride the track and control your bicycle using less than a 78" gear.

Most training for track racing is done on the road. Don't misunderstand; I want to make clear the distinction between specialty preparation and training. Certainly, Madison, match sprint and team pursuit riders must work on their techniques on the track, but this is specialized preparation as opposed to training.

Jim McCoy of Los Altos, Calif., has been a competitive cyclist and a contributor to various cycling magazines since 1969. He helped launch Bike World *in 1970 by serving as an assistant editor and consultant. In 1975 he was vice-president of the San Jose (Calif.) Bicycle Club. Aged 34 and married, Jim is a computer analyst/applied mathematician by profession.*

I'm reminded of a good example of this concept in the case of the '75 US Pan-Am 4000m pursuit team. The four riders trained exclusively at the Lake Tahoe training camp, where there is no track; when they got to Mexico, they had enough time to get in the specialized preparation needed to win the gold medal.

But now let's assume a rider plans on some track riding during the season. Starting with the winter, what training would you encourage him to do?

Peterson: I like to see riders, in the winter, put in as many miles as they have time for. This is the time of year to enjoy your bicycle riding. We are fortunate here in California to have weather that allows us to go for all-day bicycle rides Saturday or Sunday. We don't hit snow or ice, although temperatures get quite low sometimes.

I am a firm believer in low gears—63". For some reason, 63" really seems to be a great training gear, although it wasn't always accepted as such. I remember at least 10 years ago, maybe it goes back even longer than that, somebody would say, "Let's go for a ride and stay in 63", and people would say that you were out of your mind. But that's changed. I think there are more riders now who train on 63".

A 72" is a reasonable training gear although sometimes you'll be with riders in 59". I get down to a 59" myself when I'm out for a ride with a person, and rather than always dropping the other rider, or not getting a workout, I just drop the gear down and spin it up.

Offhand, I don't know of anyone who has developed into a top bicycle rider and stayed a top rider any length of time by consistently training in a high gear. I do know of riders who won racing championships in high gears, but all of these riders trained in low gears. Locally, you'll see (many time US champion) match sprinter Jack Disney out in low gears on the road. There are so many examples of top bicycle racers who train in low gears and move up for the races.

In the winter then, a rider is building stamina through mile-

age and is staying in low gears to keep leg suppleness and speed. What about weight work?

Peterson: This depends on the individual. Everybody is different. I don't think there is any way to sit down and write a training manual suitable for everybody. You can set out general rules, but basically we are all different machines. Some of us need more strength, some of us need muscle bulk, some of us need to take bulk off.

I do think, however, that most of today's young riders really neglect building up the upper torso, improving lung-chest capacity. It is hard to tell them, when they're already riding fast, that they ought to be doing maybe a bit of programmed weight training to build chest-lung capacity. Still, I definitely believe in weight training. Not necessarily heavy weights, but using low weight and high repetitions in the winter to build up stomach, back and arm strength. The weight training should be done on a regular basis like any other type of training.

Again, let me emphasize: It should be done on a regular basis, following a definite program. Sporadic weight work is near useless, if you want to progress.

Our aspiring track racer is into January and February now. What comes next?

Peterson: If a track is available, he should try to ride some training races on it. I don't say that it is a necessity, but it does help improve confidence, bike handling, and adds to one's experience.

You wouldn't be using the track to develop high speed at this time, but you should be doing a certain amount of interval work to develop (or maintain) some speed. A typical track workout might be something like the following one we use:

A 15- to 20-minute warmup (in legwarmers if temperature is below 65° F). This warmup is done in a pace line, rolling for about 15 minutes, picking up speed as we go; it gets faster and eventually turns into an informal burnout; but remember, I don't look for people at this time to be pushing so hard that they are going to be sick. This shouldn't happen.

After the warmup, everyone will rest a bit, and we will form into several groups spaced around the track and do some short jumps—probably five of these lengthening out to 100m. This loosens up everyone's legs. It is important to the effectiveness of the drill that you line people up properly. The workout leader lines the riders up close together side by side up the banking but according to jumping and sprinting ability. This gets people handlebar to handlebar, it teaches them how to ride close and to jump smooth, because if you don't jump smooth on the bank, your back wheel is going to lose traction, jump down and slow you down. But basically these warmup jumps loosen up your legs.

The workout has a good side benefit of getting new riders accustomed to the company and the techniques of riding a stiff gear bike in heavy traffic. If some riders are going faster than others on the jump, I'll move them up the bank, because the higher the bank, the harder the effort due to the steepness and the longer distance.

This gives everyone a light workout with some competition. Next we will typically get into some competition, perhaps team pursuits, or a three-mile massed start, or a controlled Madison. That would normally end the track workout.

February is a good month to start interval training on a flat road course to develop a rider's jump and sprint; in the road sessions, we will work into longer sprints, as the weeks progress.

How do you run these road intervals?

Peterson: Basically about the same as on the track; first, get the riders into comparitive ability groups. Instead of marks on on the track, you pick other landmarks for your jump start and finish points, working from short jumps to longer jumps. In these workouts, everyone is essentially in the same gear, a 63" to low 70". These gears are used through February into March.

After the series of jumps is over, you can finish off the workout with two or three half-mile sprints, which enables the riders to really wind out. If a rider is dominating a group, the workout leader moves him up to the next group and lets him race there;

it keeps riders from getting discouraged or bored.

The importance of a good jump cannot be over-emphasized. A jump is an explosion of your whole body. Not just your legs, or your arms, but your entire body—the stomach, back, and leg muscles. Most novice riders don't put everything into it. They sit back, don't want to get tired out in the jump; it's a mental thing. But in a line of riders, they have to go all out to stay with the group. First, a novice will move down in groups, but eventually he will start going all out.

To simulate the element of surprise so often encountered in an actual race, a group leader is responsible for giving a "Bang" as a signal to jump. No one goes before that bang, and when you hear it, you explode. This type of workout won't necessarily win races for you later, but it does keep other racers from getting away from you, it enables you to escape wheel-follower-free. And as far as your sprint is concerned, the greatest sprint in the world becomes ineffective in the face of top competition if you don't have that superior jump to launch it from.

Once a rider learns to explode, he needs to develop an effective body position for the move. Many riders, especially road riders, jump in too high a position—usually caused by the handlebars being too high. In general, you want to do your jumping in a deep position, where a rider's stomach, back and the hamstring muscles come into play.

A common mistake that denies this position is to jump in an extreme forward position. Some riders are exceptions to the rule and can jump well when they're way forward; however, if you're more over the saddle, you are getting your most powerful muscles fully into the effort. These are the muscles that are getting that bike moving; if you watch a kilometer man starting on the track, you see the strain that goes into it. And those who are able to get most of that power into it are getting that early advantage. On the whole, the big sprinters, the match sprinters are back over the saddle when they jump.

Recapping, in the winter, enjoy the bike, get your miles in, watch your diet and weight, do some weight training. In January-February, you'll be doing workouts as described with other riders in your club—staying on the bike, doing loosening exercises, improving your jump, and developing your sprint.

About this time the rains come. This inevitable damper plays havoc with the rigid training schedule a serious rider should be on. When this happens, you should be getting on the rollers. It keeps you loose, although you have to concentrate on working hard. There are few, if any, riders who ride rollers for any length of time and enjoy them. It is, if done properly, hard work. If you ride the rollers, ride intervals, and make it hard.

In March, we should be into competition. There should be many club races and some open training races. Keep in mind that it is still cold, so that many riders don't really loosen up, and, therefore, can't hit top speed. But the competition you are getting should be increasing your speed, and it should be conditioning you to sit on a bicycle for a while.

In March the key is speed. You'll still be taking some long rides, but toward the end of the month, you should be concentrating on speed, doing intervals at over 30 mph, team time trials at 28+ mph, and interval time trials at 25+ mph.

I want to comment on team time trialing as track training. When time trialing is mentioned, many people conjure up leg-busting Alf Engers in a 120" gear, or Beryl Burton on a 60-tooth chainring. I'm not talking about leg-busting time trials, but the type that builds speed and bike handling.

In team time trialing, each man turns 15-20 intense crank revs in a mid-70s to low 80s gear, really going as fast as he can and not staying on long, swinging crisply off. The other guys are going as fast as they can and in order to keep from losing the "train," you have to develop the techniques of riding tight, of getting efficiently into the slipstream, how to time your jump, where the echelon position is for crosswind, etc. I think that it is tremendous training. Even done on the road, it has much application to improving your track riding.

In our club races in the winter, we have an 84.9" gear limit, and there are many riders who don't even go that high. We'll probably stay around 80" and on the track we'll use perhaps 82 to 84". We don't start moving up in gears until May, unless the weather is unseasonably warm, in which case we ride higher.

How would you work motor pacing into training for track?

Peterson: First, motor pacing is not something that you do a lot of; it is useful to utilize in peaking for an event, but not as a regular thing; too much of it can run you down. To obtain best results a rider should be in top shape before he gets behind a motor. And don't content yourself just to ride behind it. Come off the motor wheel and come around. This last facet develops extra snap (acceleration) at the high speeds.

One thing you should do to tie your training program together within a season and from year to year is to program your training, keeping track of what you did, and what results you got. Keep a training diary, where you record things like weight, diet, rest, training miles/types, and results. With this record, you can modify your program, perhaps even be your own coach.

One last comment, I think a mediocre program is better than none. Even with a mediocre program, you can modify what you are doing to progress and improve as a bicycle racer.

FOUR

The Events

As mentioned in Chapter One, the list of events which constitute track racing is virtually endless. Several principal ones stand out, however. This chapter, which is the longest one in the book by far, consists of in-depth articles on these events. Those covered here are match sprint racing, time trial racing, the individual pursuit, the team pursuit, mass-start racing, tandem racing, motor-paced racing, and six-day (Madison) racing.

Although the articles vary considerably in length, each one offers a relatively detailed description of the event, its physical and psychological requirements, tactics, and valuable advice on the specific training for the event. Many of the articles were written by men who actually excelled in the particular event.

The article on match sprint racing, for example, was written by Tim Mountford, one of the finest match sprinters ever produced in the US and the most successful of the scant handful of Americans who have tried European professional racing. Tim barely lost to Leijn Loevesijn in the finals of the 1971 world professional sprint championships.

The article on the individual pursuit was written by three-time US individual pursuit champion Dave Brink.

Written by men like that, these articles could be expected to take the reader to the very heart of each event—and that's precisely what they do. Here are some excerpts to illustrate the point:

"Match sprinting is a rolling chess game which features balancing, feinting, and explosive sprints. Split-second decisions made in the heat of competition will ultimately spell victory or defeat, making the match sprint a contest of nerves and wit as well as physical skill" —Tim Mountford in "Match Sprint Racing."

"The 1000m time trial is an explosive event. The start is all important due to the short distance. If the top riders in this event are very close in top speed and endurance, then the race is decided at the starting line—the rider who gets the best start will win" —Wes Chowen in "Time Trial Racing."

"Mental toughness is that determined, aggressive attitude to push hard regardless of the circumstances—in short, the desire to win. In the team pursuit, this is translated into the desire to start fast, pull hard and finish in the twilight zone. Each rider must program himself to think of nothing but going as hard as he possibly can each time he gets on the line for the team pursuit. If you have four riders of equal ability and the technical homework has been done, the team should fly" —Dave Chauner in "The Team Pursuit."

"There must be perfect synchronization of movement during the whole race. The two men must think as one, and know exactly what action they will take in different situations. This is most important when the team is about to attack, or counter-attack. Both men have to stand on the pedals at the same instant, and they must know exactly when they are going to sit back down on their saddles after the initial jump" —John Wilcockson in "Tandem Racing."

Read on and let these men take you through the track specialties they know so well.

Match Sprint Racing

by Tim Mountford

Tim Mountford has had an outstanding 15-year career as a bike racer. As an amateur, he placed fourth (with Jack Simes) in the tandem sprint at the '69 World Championships and was 10th in the match sprint at the '68 Olympics. As a professional living in Europe, he made the top eight in each of the world professional sprint championships he entered, won Grand Prix events and was a popular six-day racer. Tim is currently a coach with the Velo Sport (Berkeley, Calif.) cycling club.

Match sprinting is a rolling chess game which features balancing, feinting and explosive sprints. Split-second decisions made in the heat of competition will ultimately spell victory or defeat, making the match sprint a contest of nerves and wit as well as physical skill

In the race itself, two, three or more riders compete over a distance of 800-1000m. If a large number of racers enter the event, a series of eliminations will be required to determine the final eight quarter-finalists.

A person interested in match sprinting should possess power and speed, and have a knack for quick reactions and creative thinking. He must have a great desire to win, and must also be willing to specialize in his training.

Physical fitness is very important in this event. If your lungs and heart aren't developed, or if your legs aren't supple enough, you won't be able to generate the explosive power a match sprinter needs.

Training is simple, assuming the rider has two or three seasons of racing in his legs and has an ingrained "feel" for pedaling. The training season starts in February, with daily rides of 30 miles in a 41 x 19 fixed gear. You should shoot for an average speed of 17-20 miles per hour on flat terrain, taking as few stops as possible.

After logging the first 500 miles, change to a 42 x 17 gear ratio for the next 500, still riding 30 miles per day. Do short (200m), all-out sprints every five miles, or about every 15 minutes.

Increase your work load in April by using a bigger gear, upping the mileage and sprinting longer distances. Specifically, get off the track or fixed-gear bike you were using and get on a road bike. Do rides of 30-50 miles (every day ideally) and lengthen your sprints to 300m. Do the sprints every other day. Also start building explosive power by doing some standing starts and some modest but fast hill work. Burst up a hill for approximately 300m at about 90 per cent of your maximum speed.

After April and into May, enter some races—if any are available. The sprinter should feel confident about entering criteriums, and winning should be his objective. However, solo or hero-type riding should be avoided. Ride in the pack and develop your leg speed, staying away from a "workhorse" type of riding.

Up to and through May you should be doing 30 miles each day, with a low but fast gear, so that you're not spinning a mile a minute but going nowhere. Use anything from a 42 x 18, 17 or 16, according to the terrain. While out on the road, make the sprints fast and snappy, because this keeps the "racehorse" feeling in the backs of your legs and in your lower back. Do your 30-mile rides every day. In addition, train on the track on Tuesdays, Thursdays, Saturdays and Sundays. (If there isn't a track around, use a safe, straight-away road course.)

Due to your road training, you should be able to hop on an 88" gear. Use an 86" gear on a slow track, such as the asphalt track in San Jose, Calif. If you're on a road course, use an 84.

Once you start training on the track in June, begin with an 88" gear. Get up to a 92 by the end of June, however, and use it through July, when the racing season begins.

The 92 is the basic gear for match sprinting throughout the world. The only time you would go to a 94 would be at high altitudes, such as at Mexico City, or on a very fast track. I once used a 94 in a professional world championship on a fast Italian track.

Note, however, that this is a standard gear ratio for Senior riders, 18 or older. Juniors should use an 88, unless the Junior is exceptionally good—say, a World Junior Team member. If he is strong and must ride a fast track, his coach may decide on a 92.

TACTICS OF MATCH SPRINTING

Match sprinting tactics can be very complex. If allowed to they become over-complex and can result in defeat. In any case, before one can employ tactics, he or she must first acquire the basics of bicycle racing. These basics are learned through several years of general racing. The rider must also develop an awareness of bicycle racing—an awareness of himself (herself), the bicycle, the competitors and the racing environment.

I think the quickest way to develop tactical sense is to go to a track which has a coach and weekly match sprint races. You will soon see that speed is the best tactic of all. This is especially true when the competitors are well matched in speed and strength. In such cases tactics are not used as much. But tactics do come into play when there is a noticeable difference in the abilities of the two riders.

There are several factors involved in race tactics. Among these factors are weather conditions, such as wind, moisture in the air and on the track, hot and cold temperatures, and the reflection of sun or light. Other factors include your opponent's strengths and weaknesses, your own strengths and weaknesses, equipment and track design.

Your first step as a competitor is to evaluate these factors. For example, what is your ability in relation to your

Stan Pantovic

The typical cat-and-mouse game of match sprint racing. Riders are Australia's John Nicholson (in the lead), '75 professional world champion, and Daniel Morelon of France, rated the top sprinter in the world today.

opponent's?

If you are a rider of lesser speed and strength than your opponent, you should take the lead position, at your own pace, before making your commitment to sprint for the finish line. Do not let your opponent get by you at this point. Try to shut down his speed just before the time you wish to start your sprint. This can be done by putting your opponent between you and the outer railing. Then, at the right moment, move him close to the rail and shut your speed off. This forces him to shut off his speed, and when he does, you take off. All this should take place around 200m or less from the finish line.

If your opponent is faster than you and you cannot obtain the lead position, you must pressure him into committing himself to a long sprint, hoping he will be a bit tired at the finish. By wind drafting on his rear wheel, you will be able to pass him just before the finish line.

One note, however. In these two examples, wind is a big factor and your opponent will try to use the wind to his advantage. Remember that it is difficult to pass someone when there is a tail wind, but easier when there is a headwind.

Should your opponent have a quicker jump or faster accelerating speed than you, be sure you are rolling at a speed that is fast enough to negate his jump. Take the lead and keep a constant check on him, especially when entering the final 300m. At this time you should be running up the speed, taking away your opponent's superior jump because the speed is already too high for the jump to be effective.

Do the opposite, however, if your jump is quicker than your opponent's. Try to catch him off guard; jump away from him and sprint for the finish line.

Generally speaking, a strong person usually will feel more at home on a large track, while a person who isn't as strong will usually prefer a smaller track. A large track is 330m (about a fifth of a mile) and a smaller track is 250m (about a sixth of a mile).

There are some tracks, however, on which it is almost impossible to pass your opponent on the last turn at full speed. In this case, you don't want to get caught too far back going into that final turn.

WIND FACTOR

Tracks are laid out so you either have a headwind down the backstretch and tailwind down the homestretch to the line, or vice-versa. If you have a lead going into the homestretch *into* a headwind, you don't want to be at full speed. You'll buck the wind and the guy behind will be taking a tremendous wind draft to pop by you into the wind using momentum you've created. In this situation, if you're in front, you have every reason to control the pace.

If there's a tailwind down the homestretch, go all out without too much worry *if you have the lead.* Don't be under speed. Use the wind to carry your speed up and finish as strong as you can. Even if your opponent is running at your wheel, you're increasing your speed all the time.

A headwind down the homestretch is a disadvantage to the rider leading—and a tailwind hurts the rider behind.

Using the wind factor on the backstretch is pure tactics. It depends on the size of the track (all outdoor tracks are 250, 333.3, 400 or 500m long). On a 250m track, you're usually already in a full sprint; but if you're leading into a headwind, you're not going full out, so the guy behind will try to pass early so he can get the tailwind advantage to the line. Track size in this situation determines when an opponent behind will make his move to pass, and you've got to be ready to react to keep your lead.

If there's a tailwind in the backstretch, the guy behind will usually lay off as much as he can, fluttering at the pedals, planning to punch at the turn to get as big a lead as he can when he hits the headwind; or it will be a duel to see who'll commit first to a leadout into that headwind.

THREE STYLES

I roughly divide opponents into three riding styles and try to be versatile enough to respond well to all three. They are: the controller, pre-concluded and the versatile.

In a match sprint, the controller always tries to dominate an opponent. He'll try to scare you, to intimidate you with his vio-

lence on the bike. He uses a repertoire of aggressive body movements to convince you he can't be pushed, can't be headed, that
he'll run over you from behind if you don't yield. He trains
himself to hold a position no matter *what* you do, as if you
haven't got a chance.

When faced with a controller you have two choices. Attack
him with aggressive moves of your own, pulling out reserves you
wouldn't otherwise have used. Or let him have his way and try
to go with him, waiting to get him when he's not looking or
when he falters.

A controller is either truly domineering with moves flowing
out of a very positive sense of his power or he may be using aggressive movement to mask insecurities about his opponent. The
good sprinter makes this distinction. You begin to realize that
very few sprinters are able to maintain the physical and mental
energy of the controller throughout a race—*somewhere* he'll
slip. He'll falter. And if you know your opponent, you'll be
able to attack this small vulnerability and when it comes time
to apply speed for the line—and he's bluffing—he'll blow up,
his legs won't go, he'll lose his breathing. His insecurity becomes
real and you go past.

If your opponent is really aggressive, you've got to trap
him any way you can. Get ahead, slow him down, bump him—
do anything to fox him out of the "power concept" he's limited to. If he loses it for a moment, the sprint may go your way.

Carl Leusenkamp was like that. I remember opposing Carl in
the Pan-Am Trials in 1967. He had me so convinced he'd
dominate me, I remember watching for his initial aggressiveness
and had to fight my impulses to give in when he started doing
something violently behind me; then he stopped thrashing side
to side and *really* charged at me. I hesitated and thought,
"Oh, Christ, here he comes." Now we were in the backstretch
and I tried to equal his speed, but he got a couple of strokes
on me and they were all he needed. He was on the inside; still
his handlebars weren't up to mine, so I tried to lean against
him to shut off his speed because I didn't have my speed up
to his, but he kept his momentum going. The way he moved

told me Carl just wasn't going to be pushed. I was at his hip trying to bump him down so we'd get a re-start, then he knocked my handlebars from under me. I went down and he won the race.

The pre-concluded rider almost always has a plan. He dopes out the environment, track condition, weather, trying carefully to calculate his opponent's moves beforehand, to get a good mental picture of where the opponent will be at any given moment during the race.

Then he comes up with an idea of what he'll do, playing the percentages that his assessments will pay off. This is okay, but it doesn't work all the time. The experienced match sprinter recognizes the "planner" by his very definite moves regardless of conditions that seem to require different adjustments. For example, he may appear very set on taking the rear position, contrary to wind conditions that would normally find both riders jockeying for a better position. You think: he's got a plan.

If you challenge a planner early enough in the race, he may drop his percentages and adjust to your moves. Or you'll watch his plan evolve and try to develop something at the last moment, when you'll challenge him, and, boom, you get three lengths on him.

I usually go with a pre-concluded rider. Save your energy. Why fight it? Unless you sense his plan will be successful because it was before, or he develops it so aggressively he comes on like a controller and you've *got* to move.

Jack Disney is a planner. And many times I've fallen into his carefully laid traps. He organizes his races *very* carefully, right down to the inch, so when his moves are good and his plan evolves, he usually leaves me sitting there.

I remember going against Jack during the 1965 National Championships in Los Angeles. He caught me going into the first turn. When we reached the banking, his plan was to "talk" me down low on the track. It worked. We were going very slowly, measuring each other and I thought he was with me all the way. Then I looked back and couldn't see him. I kept turning around, telegraphing my hesitancy, and finally saw him on the top of the banking next to the wall, but still behind me. Somehow he snuck up there.

Then he was really thrashing his pedals coming out of 12 o'clock high and there was nothing I could do but to give it everything I had for the line. We had 220m to go, and by the time we hit the stretch, he went by like a rocket ship. His plan was to get me low on the track where I couldn't get a run off as much as he could. Jack knew he had me when he reached the top of the banking and I was still low, looking around.

The versatile rider is often toughest of all. He adjusts to situations as they arise. He seldom tries to dominate or show a plan, and devises split-second tactics to counteract when he has to. Daniel Morelon is one of the most versatile riders I've ever gone against. With him, it's a real match of skill, willpower and strength. We've had some epic battles. Pure creation.

Morelon's got great speed and builds his finish calmly and decisively. So I've always gone with him, trying to put him at a disadvantage before it becomes a contest of sheer speed. If you follow him, you know he'll delay his sprint as long as possible, and if you try to make a short sprint of it and run at his wheel at the last moment, he'll pull out that reserve and you never get by. You want him full out by the time he hits that turn so you can have his wind draft as long as possible, using *his* momentum to try to pop by at the line.

Sometimes Morelon sits very calmly behind you and won't do anything. He tries to lull you to sleep. Then he makes a move to test your reaction or tries to break your morale, so I let him play with that and let him feel he's really pushing me.

When he makes his move, I increase my speed, telegraphing greater effort than I'm making. He thinks I've made a final commitment to the line, so he pushes harder and I pick it up again.

He moves, I move like an accordian and then without moving my shoulders, I turn the legs on and pull a couple of lengths on him before he reacts. Other times, I'll try to shut his speed

Two European amateurs at the finish of a closely fought sprint during a top outdoor meet in London. Note how the winner is using every last ounce of strength by pulling with straight arms on his deep, steel handlebars. Some sprint races are so close the winner isn't known until the finish photos are studied.

down, even a fraction, then jump away from him. Or he'll try to jump underneath me and I'll make a move to the left to crowd him, and maybe he'll back off slightly—I read his body movements—and try to get the advantage.

These maneuvers have worked on Morelon, but obviously not all the time, because his recovery is so quick, and acceleration so strong, he can pull you back.

One reason Morelon is so tough to beat is the training and coaching he has received. French riders, if they have any potential at all, come to Paris. I noticed this while training with

Morelon in Paris. The facilities are great—the riders even get help in finding a place to live.

As in other sports, the serious track rider needs a coach. He can't expect to get full coaching from magazines or even books like this one. In order to improve racing in the US, we have to come up with more good coaches and develop some facilities of our own. It's going to cost money, but I think the money is out there. We just have to channel it in the right direction.

Time Trial Racing

by Wes Chowen

A pilot for Continental Airlines, Wes Chowen is now retired from bike racing. But the 37-year-old southern Californian was a member of the US cycling teams in the '60 and '64 Olympic Games (where he competed as a road racer) and the '67 Pan-American Games (where he won a bronze medal in the 4000m team pursuit). His greatest achievements as a time trialist came in '61 and '67, when he set and re-set the US 30-mile and one-hour track records.

Time trial racing on the track can be broken down into three categories: the 1000m individual time trial, the 4000m time trial (women ride 3000m and professionals ride 5000m), and hour rides (or longer).

The 1000m time trial is one of the regular track events for national, world and Olympic competition. This time trial is a one-shot race; no second chances. The 4000m time trial is the qualifying event of the pursuit race, also a part of national, world and Olympic competition.

Time trials at distances over 5000m are pure record-breaking efforts not held as a regular part of any national, world or Olympic competition. These longer time trials are organized as special events when there seems to be a strong chance that a rider or team can break some existing national or world record. This long time trial is unique because of the possibilities for setting multiple records at all of the officially recognized distances up to the total distance ridden.

In 1961 I received a sanction from the Amateur Bicycle League of America to make an attempt on the US 30-mile and one-hour records. That meant a possibility of 19 records (1-15, 20, 25, 30 miles and one hour)—not counting the half or quarter-mile distances or any metric distances. In that ride I set 17 US records at the mile distance categories mentioned. I missed the one- and five-mile records.

As I recall, that ride was held at 8 or 9 o'clock in the morning to avoid the July heat that tended to soften the original bumpy asphalt surface of the Encino velodrome, which had just been built. I also used a road bike because it was more comfortable than my track bike. Due to the fact that I used a road bike my record certificate for that 1961 ride says "Road Competition Unpaced" although the ride was slightly over 193 laps *on a track.* (It seems ridiculous to have categories broken down in that way.)

In 1967 I rode 30 miles again, at Encino, and set 19 records. This time I got the five-mile record. I rode on an evening in May, under the lights. I also used a track bike with light wheels (24 spoke rear and 20 front) and the lightest tires available.

In the 1961 ride I used an 84.4 gear (50 x 16) and 170mm cranks. My times were: 10 miles—23:09.1; 25 miles—58:23.6; and 30 miles—1.10:47.2.

In 1967 I used an 88.2 gear (49 x 15) and 170mm cranks. My times on that occasion were: 10 miles—22:38.7; 25 miles—56:48.3; and 30 miles—1.08:24.2.

The 1000m time trial is an explosive event. The start is all important due to the short distance. If the top riders in this event are very close in top speed and endurance, then the race is decided at the starting line—the rider who gets the best start will win.

The top 1000m riders push big gears in this event (52 x 15, 49 x 14, 50 x 14). In 1967 I rode the 1000 primarily to improve my speed for the 4000m team pursuit. I used the same gear that I would use for an individual or team pursuit (50 x

15, 51 x 15, 48 x 14). I was able to break 1:13 for the 1000m which was respectable for a converted road rider and a pursuiter. The kilometer is very good training for team pursuiters because a good team needs a fast start.

The 4000m time trial is used in the pursuit event to select the eight (or 16) fastest competitors who will engage in match-type pursuit competition which may or may not go the full 4000m. Knowing your competition is important in deciding whether to go all out in the time trial. If you are confident of qualifying, you might save a little for the first pursuit race later that day or the next day.

Elapsed time schedules are important aids to riding a successful time trial. The time trial schedule is based on a constant lap speed after the start. The 1000m time trial presents the greatest variation in lap speeds. It requires an explosive move off the mark, followed by rapid acceleration to top speed. A large part of the muscle energy used is produced by anaerobic metabolism. This type of energy is very limited and when it is used up the muscles are full of lactic acid and practically immobilized. This is the "brick wall" that a rider usually runs into in the last 200-300m of the 1000m time trial.

The 1000m rider often rides without a prepared schedule, depending on other cues to judge his acceleration, speed and endurance.

In the 4000m pursuit, competitors will usually have a number of schedules made up in advance. Some 4000m time trials will be ridden without a schedule. The average lap times in that ride become the basis for preparing schedules for faster future rides.

The longer time trials are set up with one or maybe two schedules which are designed to bring the rider home under some existing record—personal, club, track, national or world.

PHYSICAL AND PSYCHOLOGICAL SKILLS

A fast start is very important in all of these events. It takes patience to develop this skill. It might also help to learn a little French, too, because French is the language that the starter will probably use in World Championship and Olympic competition.

Another important skill is smooth riding so that all of your energy goes into moving forward and staying within five centimeters of the pole line. Smooth riding requires strong, steady, circular pedaling.

An important psychological skill is persistance. As a recent article in *Scientific American* (June 1976) says: "The barrier to be overcome by the (athlete) who wants to be a champion is psychological; the last record set and the willingness . . . to try to break it are the determining factors for the next record."

TIME TRIAL TACTICS

Tactics in time trials can be boiled down to one item: pre-planning. The bike rider will be planning to ride at the maximum speed that he can sustain steadily over the distance—no coasting or saving energy for a sprint. This pre-planning may involve the use of schedules so the rider can know if he is ahead or behind the lap times needed to win. Possibly a 4000m pursuiter or team may not go all out in the time trial because they want to be ready for the next round of pursuit races a few hours later. A schedule will help in this case, too.

TRAINING

My training philosophy is "spin first, push later." Riding fast (20 mph or better) in small gears (67"-72") is necessary to develop endurance and supple muscles. This can be an exhausting way to ride but it pays off later when you are racing in bigger gears.

At least once during each training ride, pedal as fast as you can in this small gear for 15-60 seconds. This exercise will help smooth out your pedaling style. Choppy pedaling will cause bouncing on the bike at high leg rpm. In each road ride, do at least one practice sprint, in a big gear, to develop the strength needed to push bigger gears during the time trial.

My training schedule included three long road rides a week, every other day; each ride would be a minimum of three hours or 100 kilometers. During the racing season one of these rides would be a race on a weekend, probably a criterium of about 50 miles. On the other three or four days of the week I would spend about one to two hours on the track doing intervals (30 - 40 seconds at over 30 mph, with 30-40 seconds rest); sprints (all out for 200m with four or five minutes rest); practicing some starts and possibly doing a few practice time trials at various distances from 250m to 5000m. I wouldn't always do all of these things in one session on the track, nor would I do them in the same order each time.

Individual Pursuit

by Dave Brink

Californian Dave Brink was US national champion in the individual pursuit in '66, '67 and '68. He competed in both the individual and team pursuits in the '66 World Championships at Frankfurt, Germany, placing 19th in the individual. He had the 18th fastest time in the individual pursuit at the '68 Olympic Games, but unfortunately was disqualified for dropping below the pole line on the last lap.

In the 4000-meter individual pursuit two racers start from opposite sides of the track. The winner is the one who is able to catch his opponent or posts the fastest time for the entire distance. A standing start is used.

Initially, the field of competitors in the individual pursuit is narrowed to 16 riders (sometimes eight) through a series of individual 4000m time trials. The racers then compete head-to-head through elimination rounds.

This event lies in the territory between road racing and sprinting, so a good pursuit rider is apt to have a creditable sprint and is also capable of holding his speed for a considerable distance.

Preparation involves miles of training, with the accent on speed. One would want to maintain moderate conditioning through the winter with steady rides at an easy pace, or perhaps by going somewhat faster. By late winter and early spring, speed becomes the main target. Of course, endurance must be maintained during this period also.

A good warmup is essential before training. An effective way to warm up is to ride a low gear lightly for five miles or more, winding it up to a quick pace for the last mile or two. Aches, pains and a feeling of sluggishness may bother the rider at the beginning of the warmup. However, these should disappear as the warmup continues, leaving in their place a feeling of vitality.

A general training program for the early season could entail riding 20 miles a day at a steady, fast pace, six or seven days a week. As the cyclist finds his pace on these rides leveling off from day to day, he should add sprints to the rides — adding one more sprint every day or so. The rider should begin the sprints from the basic fast pace maintained throughout the ride and return to that pace directly after each sprint.

Sprint distances could be up to half a mile. Varying the length of the sprints can make the rider more versatile. A good target would be 20 sprints in 20 miles; the amount of effort expended here will be easily exceeded in many races. The result of such training will be good base speed, and an ability to attack and recover quickly.

Riders vary widely in the way they develop, so one person may do best on a program similar to the one described, with speedwork concentrated into 15 miles. Another rider may need 30 miles. Whichever training program is used, it should be varied according to need.

Long rides provide staying power, but are most useful when done at a quick pace, say 20 mph or more, with only one or two short stops at most. Hills are permissible if ridden properly. They should be done at a quick pace, with long hills being avoided close to race day. A safe time gap between hill climbing and a pursuit race would be a week or more, depending on the rider.

Training on the track is useful in developing sprinting ability. Individual sprints of 200m or more, with 10 or 15 minutes rest between them, develop the strength needed to apply a burst of speed for a short distance. Time trials of 1000-2000m and 4000m team pursuits also help develop speed. In addition, they

Robert George

US star Mary-Jane (Miji) Reoch competing in the women's individual pursuit at the '74 World Championships in Montreal. She was a silver medalist in the event at the '75 World Championships.

provide a good method for determining the pace one is capable of maintaining. Riding an individual 4000m pursuit in training, however, can be physically and psychologically exhausting, so it is not a viable training method for frequent use.

Motor pacing can be helpful for pulling speed out of the rider. The ride should be fast and pedal action light. A session of motor pacing should last 15-30 minutes at most, and should be done perhaps twice a week. Be careful not to become overly dependent on motor pacing, however.

Although all types of road and track races are good training for pursuiters, the racer should not ride in too long and exhausting an event close to the day of his pursuit race.

Whatever training methods are used, the pursuiter needs a balance of speed and endurance. The rider can arrive at this balance by identifying his strong points and weak points from time to time, and planning his training accordingly.

In a pursuit race itself, the riders are across the track from each other and there is less maneuvering for position than in other types of racing. However, there are tactical games that can be played.

As the riders approach their starting positions, they are sweating lightly. They tighten their toe straps as their starters hold bikes and riders steady. Trainers stand ready with watches to give the riders lap times and keep them on schedule.

After a few deep breaths and a moment's observation of the opponent, the command sounds, "Riders ready, starters ready," and the gun fires.

Consider yourself one of the racers at that moment. You apply the power, fast. Getting up to a smooth, steady rate, you pace yourself so you'll have enough energy to maintain speed throughout the race. Hold that pole line and keep low; now quickly glance at your opponent. What is his position? Does he start fast and finish slow, ride at a steady pace, or finish fast?

Try to get a little lead — you'll be that much ahead and you'll get a bit of a psychological advantage as well.

What is your opponent doing? Is he struggling or in control? Is his apparent struggle a bluff? Watch it! Four laps left now. You have lots of energy and a good lead; accelerate slightly and increase the lead. Two laps left — now pour it on, all the way to the finish line.

That is how a pursuit ride might go, but there are different objectives in the various rides during an individual pursuit competition. In the first ride, the time trials which determine the riders who continue into the elimination rounds, the goal is to get the fastest possible time. The advantage of having the fastest time — in addition to qualifying — is that after the time trials, the man with the fastest time rides against the man with the eighth fastest time; the second fastest rides against the seventh fastest, and so on. Therefore, a quick first ride can mean an easier second ride. And an easier second ride allows the rider to conserve energy for his next race.

Likewise, if the semi-final seedings are determined by fastest quarter-final times, the racer will try to post a fast time in the quarter-finals, thus setting up the likelihood of an easier semi-final ride.

Whichever way the race is ridden, the pursuiter should be able to ride a steady line around the track. He should not waver upward, increasing the distance he must travel, nor should he waver downward, thus shortening his distance and risking disqualification. His position on the bicycle should cut down on wind resistance but present no restriction to breathing.

Many riders use pre-planned schedules to keep themselves on a pace which will enable them to cover the distance in the least amount of time. This can be a great time trial device, but it can break down when the rider is confronted by an opponent across the track. For example, a rider may surprise himself and exceed his best time when pressed by an opponent. Or a rider with a fast finish but a slow overall ride could beat a rider with a faster overall ride by hanging back slightly, then applying his fast finish unexpectedly, thereby catching the opponent by surprise. Similarly, a rider with a slow finish had better gain plenty of distance before the last few laps.

So what is best? Try to lead and maintain that lead, or hang back and try to sprint a bit faster at the end? The answer to that question is another question: which position can your opponent function from best? Is he upset by having the opposing rider only two yards down but holding the pace? Does he panic and lose concentration when he is a couple of yards down? You must be able to determine what the man across the track is doing, and what he likes to do.

A pursuit race may wind up being ridden in numerous ways, and is potentially very exhausting. The race is short enough so that a large energy reserve is available for the ride, but long enough for the rider to develop an oxygen debt. Therefore, breathing is very important in the pursuit. The better the oxygen intake is balanced with work output, the faster the ride will be, and the easier it will be for the rider to recover afterward.

The gear used in the race must suit the track and the rider's condition. Too big a gear can be heavy and difficult to bring up to a steady, light spin. Too small a gear can leave a racer unable to maintain a fast enough pedal rate for the duration of the ride.

These, then, are the basic requirements for a good pursuit ride; a good training background, a knowledge of your own abilities in speed and endurance, a gear matched to the conditions, and the ability to determine what your opponent is doing and how you will respond to it.

The Team Pursuit

by Dave Chauner

Now retired from racing, Dave Chauner is a vastly experienced team pursuit cyclist, having ridden on national championship teams as well as internationally. Late in his career he switched from track to road racing. Last year he became the first American to win a stage of the Tour of Britain (the so-called Milk Race). Dave is a frequent contributor to Velo-News *and is the regular announcer at the Trexlertown (Penn.) velodrome.*

The team pursuit is one of the most specialized events in cycling.

The race itself lasts less than five minutes, but during that time there is no margin for error, no time to think, and no room for anything except total concentration.

The biggest question facing the aspiring state competitor, the seasoned international veteran and the US Olympic Team coach is, "How do I get four individuals to program themselves to click as a team for 4000 meters of flat-out effort?" The problem obviously doesn't have a simple solution, as any American or top international coach would be quick to point out.

There are, however, a few observations that I have made during the last several years that may shed a little light on the subject of team pursuit.

First is the obvious but often overlooked fact (in the US, anyway) that every pursuit team is completely different. What is right for the German team won't work for the Danes or the Italians. And if the Dutch prepared like the French, they might lose to the Americans.

Every country (or state or region) has different resources of talent, making it nearly impossible to achieve the same success by using the same methods.

Thus, it is ridiculous for us to pick up the latest cycling magazine from Europe, read that all four members of the West German team have the same body structure, and conclude that the prime ingredient for success is equal height and weight.

It's a great idea if you have 50 talented pursuiters who are all five feet, 11 inches tall. But here in the US, we are lucky to have *two* talented pursuiters of the same height and weight, let alone 50. So we are working on a much smaller scale, where the big chore is simply to find the talent, rather than select from the talented.

What talents must a fine team pursuiter have? And how can we be sure he will click with three others of equal ability? As I see it, the team pursuiter (as well as any racing cyclist for that matter) must possess three basic characteristics: physical ability, mental toughness and technical expertise.

PHYSICAL ABILITY

The prime physical ingredient for any team pursuiter must be speed.

When you are riding in a breakaway in a road race and the pace suddenly leaps up two or three miles per hour, try to see who is pulling. If he's making you hurt, he's got potential — and if he's doing it in a 52 x 16 or a 52 x 15, sign him up immediately! (If he is in a 53 x 14 or above, he may not have the *souplesse*, or pedal action, of the true team pursuiter.)

Looking for potential team pursuiters in a road race is a little shaky, however, so go down to the track and watch a few races. The riders who are winning fast team races, fast miss-and-outs, and fast scratch races are potentially excellent team pursuiters.

Robert George

They will be riding aggressively, have the ability to close gaps or pull in a breakaway, and will often win a sprint or two. Generally, they will be making the race too hard for the pure sprinters and too fast for the roadmen.

A talented, lean kilometer man is often the strongest member of a fast pursuit team. Lumpy kilometer men like Pierre Trentin are horrendous in the team pursuit, but very fit, all-round type kilo men are excellent. Multi world champion Niels Fredborg is an asset to any team, as was Jackie Simes, an extremely fast and fit all-round track rider.

Usually a good individual pursuiter can help a team. But selecting the top four individual pursuiters exclusively is like expecting a work horse to outrun a race horse because the former looks stronger than the latter.

Often one of the best members of a pursuit team shows nothing as a specialist in anything else. Mike Hiltner, member of the US team that competed in the 1971 Pan-American and 1972 Olympic Games, is a case in point. Slow in the kilo and terrible as an individual pursuiter, he was able to fit extremely well in the fastest team pursuit ever ridden by Americans — a 4:28 in Cali, Columbia. That kind of speed is only achieved by a very fast and light pedaling action, which is Mike's style.

An all-round, fast track rider is the man to start with in building a pursuit team. If he is aggressive and attacks time after time in a fast race, he will usually make a good team pursuiter.

MENTAL TOUGHNESS

We all know how important mental attitude is to success. In a highly competitive environment the proper attitude can make the difference between giving that little extra for victory or settling for being another also-ran.

Mental toughness is that determined, aggressive attitude to push hard regardless of the circumstances — in short, the desire

Team pursuit action at the East Point, Ga., velodrome. The event, which the author calls "one of the most specialized in cycling," requires four riders to mesh together smoothly "for 4000 meters of flat-out effort."

to win. In the team pursuit this is translated into the desire to start fast, pull hard and finish in the twilight zone. Each rider must program himself to think of nothing but going as hard as he possibly can each time he gets on the line for a team pursuit. If you have four riders of equal ability and the technical homework has been done, the team should fly.

Since we are dealing with a team event, the mental makeup of the unit is composed of four distinct parts which must complement each other. No one individual can have a "you guys have got to come through for me" attitude. When that exists, resentment builds up among the other members; the team becomes polarized and out on the track the event becomes a blow-off session. Sometimes this makes for faster times but usually it results in rocket-through pulls which invariably reduce a team to rubble.

The most effective team pursuit rider is the one who can see the event in terms of "we," is mentally tough enough to always push himself to the limits, and can maintain a sense of humor even when the team doesn't click.

TECHNICAL EXPERTISE

No pursuit team can perform without a certain amount of technical expertise. Obviously, the higher the level of competition, the more nearly perfect must be the technique in order for the team to win. When discussing technique it is necessary to look at three aspects: preparation technique, competition technique, and management technique.

From other events in cycling we know how important preparation or training is to top performance. The team pursuit probably requires a good deal more time spent in highly specialized training designed to mold four individuals into a polished unit. If you have the right men, they will already be fit enough and fast enough; the only thing left to do is to put the icing on the cake.

A coach should know who his four men will be early in the season and have them racing and training always with the team pursuit in mind. Early road form is essential with plenty of early season training miles and road races, remembering at all times that the miles should be ridden aggressively. Sitting in for three-quarters of the race with only one or two well-timed efforts may win the race but it won't make a better team pursuiter. Go for primes, attack frequently, always stay near the front. In short, try to win the race in the most aggressive manner possible. Stay away from monstrous gears and remember that a team pursuiter must be a fast and light pedaler.

About 1½-2 months before the important event (I will assume the team is preparing for the Nationals), all the riders should be racing weekly on the track (if possible, of course) and limiting their road racing to fast criteriums up to 100 km. Two or three times per week everyone should try to get together for some team workouts. If a track is available, start doing the following workout twice per week:

- 20 minute warmup, starting slow, finishing at top speed.
- roll easily, or get off the bike and rest 10 min.
- 2000m timed team pursuit from standing start. Ride it at race speed.
- rest 10 minutes.
- 2000m timed team pursuit from flying start.
- rest 20 minutes.
- spend 45 minutes to an hour in individualized training. Practice some starts, break off into teams for a training Madison, etc.

It is a good idea to ride one full 4000 each week to get a measure of improvement and an indication of where the work is needed.

If a track is not available for training, find a long flat section of smooth road, ride track bikes, and come as close to the described workout as possible.

In all workouts, a gear very close to your race gear is essential. The 49 x 15 or 50 x 15 are perfect; the maximum gear to use in the National Championships will be 51 x 15. Most international teams use no higher than a 50 x 15 or 51 x 15 on super fast tracks and have no trouble finishing under 4:35 (they pedal fast!).

In the last two weeks before the National Championships, try to get together nearly every day for short, fast team workouts. These should be 30-50 miles of road riding with low gears in the morning or evening, in addition to the pursuit workout.

Taper off on all hard riding a week before the event, but still ride every day. Riding behind a motorcycle at 30 mph for 60-90 minutes each day is excellent. Also, plenty of rest and regular diet are critical at this time.

Now we come to the point where all the training and other preparation must be put together for the event itself. Competition technique and strategy should be gradually determined through close observation of the riders during training.

If one man is exceptionally strong, exploit his strength by having him pull on the windy side of the track, or have him do an extra turn at the front. If the team is made up primarily of fast kilometer or sprint types, half-lap pulls for each man might be best. If the riders are individual pursuit types, have them each pull full laps. If one man is weaker, make sure he starts in third or fourth position, doesn't have to pull against the wind, and toward the end of the race takes a half lap instead of a full lap pull.

In choosing the man who will start in first position, remember he must be strong (a start takes a lot out of you), he must be consistent and reliable, and he must have a fast start (but not necessarily the fastest). If one man has a slow start, have him ride in the fourth position so he has plenty of time to fall into line.

Always remember that the goal for a pursuit team is to ride as fast as possible with the least amount of fluctuation in speed. The worst thing that can happen to a team is having a man shoot through too fast to begin his pull. He blows everyone off in the first 50 yards and causes everyone to crash into him in the last 50.

If the pace must be picked up, pick it up gradually, allowing the man who has just swung off to get back on without having

Rodale Press Photo

"If the pace must be picked up, pick it up gradually, allowing the man who has just swung off to get back on without having to chase until his next pull." The '75 US Pan-Am team in action.

to chase until his next pull. The last half of any man's turn at the front should be faster than his first half.

When switching off, the front man begins to drift up slightly as he approaches the turn, enabling the second man to start moving inside and get a clear view of the pole line. The second man can then begin his pull smoothly, avoiding any erratic movements.

The time for the lead man to swing off is when he is far enough into the turn so that full advantage of the banking can be used. On a steeply banked track this is no problem; the front man will continue almost straight ahead when the turn approaches. This shoots him right up the banking and, with practice, he will know the exact moment to cut back down to bring him within inches of the last man. On a shallow track, however, the front man must be careful not to get too far up on the bank because there is no slope to shoot him back down. In either case, each man must perfect his technique so he can get back in line quickly, rather than having to chase his teammates halfway down the straight before he catches up.

If at all possible, serious contenders for the National title should spend the week before the race working on technique at the track. A lot of practice is needed to get a feel for switching off at 30+ mph. This practice also helps teammates to get to know each other well, and to know what to expect from each other under all circumstances.

The last item I will comment on is potentially one of the most important for any pursuit team. It is the management or coaching technique that must go into any team event.

We all know that cyclists, especially US cyclists, are highly individualistic athletes who do not fit into the "rah rah" team spirit, American sport mold. If they did, they would be pitching or tackling instead of sprinting or pursuiting. With this in mind, it is essential to have a coach or manager who understands that he must be very delicate in trying to mold four cyclists into one unit. Often the riders can coach themselves if one or two of them have the necessary experience and leadership ability for the job.

Almost as important as proper coaching techniques is proper management of a pursuit team. The best person to have is someone who can do the following things well: operate a stopwatch, drive a motorcycle, work on bikes, organize workouts, maintain high morale, and pump up tires. In short, you need a good worker who wants to see his team win.

Mass-Start Racing

by John Wilcockson

Bike World's international editor, John Wilcockson wrote the first chapter of this book. This article is the first of four he has contributed to this chapter. As a Category I rider in England, John competed in road races, time trials and on the track. As a journalist, he has covered the top cycling events, including the World Championships and the Tour de France.

Mass-start racing is a common, and spectacular, part of most track meets. It's also very popular with riders since it's ideal for non-specialists – and many riders fall into that category.

There are various types of mass-start races, including five- and 10-mile scratch events, points races (where the distance is usually five miles) and devil-take-the-hindmost (or elimination) races.

As yet, there are no mass-start races in the Olympics or World Championships, but a 10-mile mass start is the traditional climax of the US National Championships and there is a 20-kilometer (12½-mile) mass-start in the Commonwealth Games. There is also a 20-km mass-start race in the British Championships.

Sprinters, pursuiters and roadmen all have an opportunity to shine in races of this type. Consequently, there is a constant battle of strategies. The roadmen will want to break away as early as possible to split up the field, and maybe establish a successful break. The pursuiters will want to keep the pace fast

in order to blunt the finishing speed of the sprinters. And the sprinters will want to abort as many attacks as possible so that the overall pace is reduced, giving them a better chance to win the finishing sprint.

Hence, this can be an absorbing event, both for spectators and riders, particularly when a championship is at stake. The Commonwealth Games event, for instance, has many of the elements of a road race because of the participation of teams from the leading countries — England, Australia, New Zealand, etc. The pattern of racing is decided by these teams, who each try to get their best sprinter to the closing stages of the race as efficiently as possible or alternatively attempt to get a man away in a winning break. The result is that individual riders from smaller countries often have the chance to take advantage of the big-team maneuvering to get away in their own attacks. This sometimes results in unexpected placings.

Such opportunism is also possible in a race without teams, because there will always be a number of race favorites who will watch each other like hawks to avert being caught by unexpected attacks. They frequently get their way, of course, with the race following a more traditional pattern: a series of attacks and counter-attacks, with a select group reaching the closing laps after the weaker riders have been lapped or left behind.

The qualities of a good 10-mile (or 20-km) rider will be skill, stamina and speed — skill to know when to attack, and which attacks to counter, which riders to chase; stamina to be able to continually make high-speed bursts, closing gaps or instigating breaks; and speed to outsprint whoever is left with you at the end — whether it is only one rider or the whole pack.

It's because of these varied demands that mass-start track

(Previous photo) An Intermediate mass-start race at the '73 National Championships in Northbrook, Ill. (Right) Jeff Saunders leads Gibbie Hatton in a Junior race at the '74 Nationals, also in Northbrook. (Both photos by Robert George)

racing is such a good training event for roadmen — as long as they don't hide themselves away in the middle of the pack. Another excellent race for them is the points race, in which a rider has to remain constantly near the head of the string to be sure of having the chance to score points. These are awarded to the first three, four or five riders across the line on every lap, or every second lap, depending on the size of the track.

The points race is one of the events in the Junior World Championships, and is also included as part of the junior omnium championship at the US Nationals. It is not an Olympic or Senior World Championship race.

The necessary qualities required to be a successful points rider are basically the same as those one needs to be a good 10-miler, but the tactics employed are much different. The race is not won at the finish; it is won at the end of each points lap. This means that every attack is of importance.

One of the best tactics to employ in a points race is to go with all the early breaks in an attempt to build up a useful tally of points. This gives a rider a psychological advantage over his opponents and allows him to stay quietly on the defensive later while the others endeavor to win points of their own. It is sometimes surprising how few points can constitute a winning total.

Another tactic that can prove successful is to pin all your hopes on one major effort during the middle part of the race. Wait until an attack has been caught, and then put in a rapid counter to open up a big lead. With luck, you will be able to stay clear for two or three scoring laps — and perhaps total a winning number of points. The thinking behind this strategy is that the early attackers will be too tired to chase and that the sprinters will be reserving their efforts to win points in the bunch sprints, hoping that they can pick up enough points in this way to win overall.

The other type of mass-start event is the devil-take-the-hindmost, which is an excellent spectator event, although it's not too pleasant for riders who get eliminated in the early laps. Devils can be particularly entertaining in the fabric of a six-day race, in which the riders have great scope for self-expression. Consequently, the race will become like a music-hall routine — the villain will be the aloof professional concentrating on winning; the hero will be the showman who just manages to avoid being eliminated each lap by the width of his rear tire; and the comic will be the character who perhaps assumes the role of the referee and dramatically points out which rider should be eliminated.

In a more serious elimination race, the judging is one of the most difficult tasks for track officials because it is much more difficult to decide who is last over the line in a big pack than who is first. For this reason, riders should avoid staying near the back — or, rather, they should concentrate on maintaining a position at the front, out of the danger area.

Staying at the rear of the pack *can* prove to be a winning tactic — if you are strong and confident enough to outsprint the other tailenders each lap. But it is a far more positive approach to gamble on making breaks from the front. For example, a break of three riders could get away in the first part of the event, leaving the others to take up the chase or face certain elimination. This is just one of the many situations which can make devils such enthralling races.

No specific type of training is necessary for mass-start track racing because every race is different. On one occasion, it could be the sprinters who win the prizes; on another, it could be the pursuiters or the roadmen who come out on top.

Tandem Racing

by John Wilcockson

To see a tandem bike being propelled at over 40 miles per hour around a steeply banked track by two powerful sprinters is to see one of the most awe-inspiring sights in track racing. Unfortunately, it is becoming an increasingly rare sight. The tandem sprint has been dropped from the Olympic Games, a move which will jeopardize the event's continuity at the world championship level as well. (In fact, tandem racing was not introduced to the World Championships until 1966, although its life as an Olympic event extended back to 1908.)

The rules for the tandem sprint are the same as for the individual match sprint event, but the tactics are considerably different. The usual advantage of being at the back in a sprint race is not as important here because a tandem pair literally has eyes in the back of its head — the rider on the back (sometimes referred to as the stoker) is able to keep a permanent watch on the other tandem. Consequently, there are rarely any standstills in this 1500-meter event, and the parrying for positions is a continuous process, building up to the final sprint, which usually begins when there's about 400m to go.

The build-up and the sprint are much longer than in individual sprinting because of the tandem's greater inertia. No instant speed or acceleration is available, and once the initiative has been taken by one team, they must follow their effort through to its conclusion. A typical race would go like this:

The twosome in front want to stay in the lead so they set a fairly steady pace, keeping close to the top of the banking. In this position, they are constantly ready to attack by diving down the banking, and they are ideally placed to control their opponents. If the opposing team tries to go by on the outside, the front team can quickly move to the right before the attack is fully under way; and if the opposing team attempts to drop down on the inside, the leaders should again be able to close the door with an immediate dive of their own.

Once the final sprint is underway, the team that takes the lead rides at about 90 per cent effort until starting a second kick in the back straight, where the other team must make its bid for the lead. It is almost impossible to get by in the finishing straight in tandem racing, unless it is a particularly long track. That is because the longer length of a tandem bike, combined with the faster speeds that are attained, means it takes a lot longer to pass.

It takes great strength to sustain these long sprints and to control the latent power of a tandem. When you watch a top class tandem sprint event, you can almost feel the power being generated as two machines swoop round the final banking at top speed. It is not an event for novices. The ideal combination of riders is a seasoned sprinter on the front and a sprinter/kilometer rider at the back. The two men should be of similar height (for better streamlining), with the heavier rider steering (to make the weight of riders and bike more evenly balanced).

A tandem pair should have similar temperaments as well as complete confidence in each other. One of the best teams on record has been the French combination of Daniel Morelon, world sprint champion, and Pierre Trentin, former world kilometer champion. But they have often failed to live up to their potential, mainly because of their differing temperaments. Morelon is controlled and conscientious, while Trentin is volatile and liable to lose confidence in his own ability. Even so, they have won both the World and Olympic titles, recording a remarkable 9.83-second last 200m in the 1968 Mexico final (that's over 45 mph!).

It is not necessary to be a champion sprinter to make a good tandem rider, and time has shown that the most consistent performances come from a pairing of less talented individual sprinters. They can make up for any lack of inherent speed by perfecting their coordination and technique through long hours of practice.

For instance, there must be perfect synchronization of movement during the whole race. The two men must think as one, and know exactly what action they will take in different situations. This is most important when the team is about to attack, or counter-attack. Both men have to stand on the pedals at the same instant, and they must know exactly when they are going to sit back down on their saddles after the initial jump. Their actions should be smooth and fluid; such style will come only after that long period of preparation.

The specialized training required for tandem racing should begin at least a month prior to the first meet. The two riders will already be in racing trim, so the main purpose of the training is to adapt their styles to the longer machine. If possible, the pair should use a road tandem for training runs of 30-40 miles, repeated two or three times a week. This will develop a familiarity with each other's style, and will also be an ideal opportunity for practicing jumps and putting in longer sustained efforts of about one kilometer. The tandem should be fitted with a fixed wheel of 90-96 inches; therefore, as flat a route as possible should be selected for the training rides.

On the track, there should again be two or three sessions a week, depending on how frequently the two riders can get together. If there are other tandem pairs in the area, races should be arranged during track league meets. The pattern of training will be the same as for individual sprinting: warmup, practice jumps, motor-paced, intervals, etc. Again, emphasis should be on building up coordination of effort, so that the two riders act as one. A coach is important, both for getting the tandem pair's 200-meter times and helping them perfect their style. Gear size for track training should be in the 100-105 inch range, depending on the smoothness of the track. Of course, tires and wheels will be heavier than those to be used in competition.

For racing, the gear size will be pushed up another four to five inches, and wheels will probably be spoked 36 (front) and 40 (back) for an average pair of riders. The importance of well-built wheels with tires very firmly shellacked cannot be emphasized too strongly. A crash on a tandem traveling at 45 mph may be an exciting spectacle for spectators, but it can be a frightening experience for the riders.

If you get the chance to watch (or compete in) tandem sprinting, make sure you take it. There must be a bright future for almost any serious pair of riders in tandem racing, which definitely needs an injection of new blood and spectator interest if it is to survive in the coming years.

Motor-Paced Racing

by John Wilcockson

Motor-paced racing is the fastest and most specialized form of track cycling. The "stayers" (as the competitors are known) ride bikes that have small front wheels and very big gears. These riders are paced by large, old-fashioned looking motorbikes driven by men wearing thick leathers from head to toe. There is a certain mystique attached to the event. For one thing, it must be one of the few athletic contests in which world championship medals are awarded to "non-competitors." Both pacer and rider are given joint awards.

It may seem sacrilege to award medals to motorcyclists in a cycling championship, but anyone who has seen motor-paced racing knows that a good pacer can mean the difference between success and failure. In fact, it is not an oversimplification to say that the pacer provides the brains, the rider the legs of the team.

It takes many years of experience to make a good pacer, and the best ones were stayers themselves before taking over the front position. A pacer has to be an expert judge of speed and tactics. He must be able to compensate for any wind — knowing when to use the accelerator, and when to use the brake in order to give his rider a smooth pace. And he must know when and where to attack, making sure the acceleration is gently progressive.

The pacer actually stands up on the motorbike so that he offers as big a wind break as possible. It also means that he is closer to his rider, and is thus in a better position to hear any instructions – *Allez!* (to go faster) and *Ho!* (to ease the pace). He wears a helmet, of course, but it is fitted with rear facing "ear pockets" to permit better hearing.

An important feature of the pacing machine is the metal roller bar fitted at its back extremity. This roller controls the distance between the rider's front wheel and the "wind break." The roller is fixed at hub level, and its distance from the motorbike's back wheel depends on the type of track being ridden.

The further away the roller is from the motorbike, the slower will be the actual speed of the stayers. If the velodrome is wide with long curves and a steep banking, the judges will declare conditions "safe," meaning that the roller can be closer to the pacing machine to allow higher speeds. The roller will be fixed further back when conditions are not as safe – for instance, if the track has a bumpy surface, shallow bankings, tight turns, poor transitions, etc.

Average speeds in motor-paced racing are usually between 70 and 80 km/hr (44-50 mph). This means that a complex pattern of air currents is established at track level: near-vacuums behind each of the, say, six pacers and much turbulence and buffeting further back. It is because of this that you will rarely see two stayer combinations racing close together – the risk of being blown back by the "wall" of air is too great.

The best tactic to employ is to take the lead, so that the whole race can be controlled from the front. The rider can then continue at the pace he feels is comfortable, and he is in a position to beat off any challenges by accelerating. In addition, the longer the challenger is riding against the "wall" the more tired he is likely to get by the latter stages of the race.

The stayer's bike is specially built to extremely tight specifications. Tubing is extra strong and the front forks are

Pacer and rider during the motor-paced race at the '74 World Championships in Montreal. The pacer stands up on the motor-bike to provide the greatest possible wind break. Average speeds in motor-paced racing are usually 44-50 mph.

unique because they face backward, instead of forward, to accommodate the small (21 inches diameter) front wheel. The small front wheel enables the rider to stay closer to the pacing machine. Other unusual features of the bike are the fat saddle (with a steel supporting rod), the shallow steel handlebars (with stem support) and the special front tire (which is "wrapped" to the rim).

Safety and comfort are the reasons for the strange shape and accessories of a stayer's bike. There are enormous stresses exerted on machine and rider by the bankings, which one hits eight times a minute when travelling around a 333.33m track at 80 km/hr. On a bumpy track, the pressures are further accentuated, causing the bike to literally bounce around the track. Hence the need for a soft saddle and the added strengthening.

Motor-paced races cover considerable distances. The professional world title race was 100 km long until recently, when the event was reduced to one hour's duration; the amateurs race over 50 kms. In fact, many riders fit small water bottles on their 'bars and periodically sip from the plastic straw to replace some of the liquid lost in perspiration. It is dangerous to take your hands off the 'bars, so a conventional bidon is not feasible.

Before a race begins, riders draw for order of start, and the pacers put on large body numbers to indicate their position in the line. After the motorbikes are push-started and cough into action, the pacers circle the track until they are in the correct order, and in fairly close single file. Meanwhile, the stayers mount their machines, also lined up in the correct starting order on the finishing straight.

When the judges are satisfied that everything and everyone is ready, the gun fires and handlers run, pushing the bikes until the riders have enough speed to set their big gears into motion. In unison, the trainers will all throttle back on their engines, allowing each rider to slip in behind his pacing motor. It is an advantage to be drawn in the front position, because the man at the back could find himself as much as half a lap down on the leader almost as soon as the race gets going.

However, many an experienced rider prefers to be in a trailing position, where he can sit back, matching the pace of those in front, and see exactly how each rider is performing. In this position, he can ride himself in, reserving his efforts until he is ready to accelerate. As mentioned earlier, the tactics of motor-paced racing are very much controlled by the wind pressures that are set up — and it is not uncommon to see a rider blown completely away from his pacing motor by the "wall" from the combination in front.

Riders are not permitted to overtake on the inside of the stayers line — the blue line painted around the track a third of the distance from the inside. So all challenges have to be made around the top of the banking. To see a pair of expert stayers battling it out at over 50 mph, thundering around the bankings, is an unforgettable sight.

Over the years, there has been much speculation about trainers (the men who ride the motorbikes) taking bribes and fixing the results of championship events. There was undoubtedly a lot of truth in the stories: enough, anyway, for the *Union Cycliste Internationale* to change the regulations to make it compulsory for both rider and pacer to be of the same nationality. This was initiated to stop the leading trainers, who control the winter season of indoor motor-paced racing, from hiring out their services to the highest bidder and making him a likely winner. The new system is designed to give every competitor a fair chance to show his true form. This is fine in theory, but it can mean that a rider from a country without regular motor-paced racing has to race behind a less-skilled trainer, and is denied the chance to compete on equal terms.

Motor-paced racing is such a specialized branch of track cycling that few men can find success in it without complete dedication. This means that these riders are not likely to move out of their strange world and have equal success in conventional racing. There are exceptions, but the real specialist will invariably come out on top in motor-paced racing.

The demands of the event are great — the rider must be supple enough to spin a high gear at a good cadence, and must have sufficient stamina to sustain this high level of performance for an hour.

Due to these contrasting demands, preparation for stayer racing is not simple. There must be a broad base of road miles on which to build and perhaps many long sessions of interval training to develop the necessary speed. But the major requirement is access to regular motor-paced training (on the road, as well as the track). It is only during periods of this type of training that the proper combination of technique, position, breathing and endurance can be perfected.

Six-Day(Madison)Racing

by John Wilcockson

If an American sports fan suddenly found himself in the center of a European six-day arena, it is unlikely he would know what was happening. He would see a confusing number of cyclists on the track — some racing flat out, others coasting at the top of the banking. Lights would be flashing and numbers constantly changing on an electronic scoreboard.

Some of the spectators would be cheering and stamping their feet in the bleachers; others would be munching hot dogs, swilling beer and listening to a brass band in the infield. And above it all, an announcer (probably speaking Dutch or German) would be booming over loudspeakers, giving details of which teams were leading by how many laps, which team had the most points, etc. . .

Six-day bike racing is as much a social outing as it is a sports event — and there are some serious cyclists and coaches who say the six-day is only a pale imitation of real bike racing. If they are only interested in athletic endeavor, that viewpoint may be valid. But sport today has to be spectacular if it is to be a commercial success, and six-day races are spectacular. In that respect they have certainly come a long way since the first six-day bicycle race was held in London, England at the end of the 19th century. That event was about as spectacular as a non-stop dance marathon.

The first six-day events (competitors didn't ride on the seventh day because that was the Sabbath) were of the race-till-you-drop variety. It wasn't until they originated the concept of two-man teams (one team member on the track at all times) that this specialized branch of cycle racing became a real success. That first two-man event was promoted in New York's Madison Square Garden; hence the term Madison racing used in the English language, and the French term *a l'Americaine* meaning "American style."

Before World War II, six-day racing was very popular in the United States, but those times are gone. This was demonstrated a few years back when attempts to re-introduce professional six-day races to the US proved futile.

Successful modern events featuring top European riders have been held in Montreal and Toronto, but it is the bike fans from the European communities of these Canadian cities that mainly support the promotions.

However, there are signs that Madison racing is becoming more popular with American amateurs. Witness riders such as Roger Young competing successfully in amateur six-day races on the indoor tracks of Europe.

Over the years, many supplementary events have been added to the basic framework of the six-day. These include sprints, handicaps, elimination races, motor-paced and points races. They were originally introduced to give spectators better value for their money, and to relieve riders from the monotony of constantly circling the track in all-day Madison competition.

In a modern "six," therefore, there are only about two hours of Madison racing each day, with the other events, possibly including an amateur one-hour race, making up the remainder of the eight-hour schedule. In other words, a six-*day* is more correctly a six-*night* (racing usually ends at midnight, or later), which is a more practical situation for all concerned and gives rise to much faster racing.

Now that you have a better impression of what is included in

John Wilcockson

Two greats of track racing are shown executing a Madison change in a six-day race. Nearest the camera is Dutch colossus Peter Post, winner of more six-day events than any other man in history. His partner here is Belgium's Ferdinand Bracke, former world pursuit champion and holder of the world hour record.

a six-day event, we will focus on the Madison. Rules vary from country to country, and there is no one standard distance. Tactics change from one size of track to another. Perhaps the best way to describe a Madison, therefore, is to look at an imaginary race.

It is common for about a dozen teams to compete in a six-day race, but to keep things as simple as possible, let's say we have six teams (A to F) in the race. Each team has two riders and the race will cover 200 laps of a 250m track, a distance of 50 km. The winning team will be one that:

a) Scores the most points in the sprints contested every 10th lap and finishes within the same lap as the first team; or

b) Finishes more than a lap clear of any other team, whatever the number of points that team may have scored.

On big tracks (333m or larger), where it is almost impossible to gain a complete lap on the other leading teams, the sprints for points become all important. On small tracks of 200m or less, it is much easier to "take laps," making points less important. On medium-sized tracks (the 250m in our example), both the laps and the points have equal significance.

At the start of the race, one rider from each team lines up while the other riders slowly circle the track on the outside. The gun fires and the first six move into action, swapping pace much the same as would a pursuit team. This continues until the main pack closes on the slower moving group of riders, who are ready to drop down the banking, to be relayed into the race by their partners. The latter will in turn be relayed into the race following their lap of relaxed, slow riding.

For one man to hand over the pace to his teammate (to relay him), he must ride alongside and push him forward. This is called a "Madison sling," or simply a "change." It is normally effected by a rider on the inside grabbing hold of a pad fitted into a narrow pocket on the left hip of the other man's shorts, and throwing him into the action.

In our imaginary race, all six teams complete their changes almost simultaneously and there are six new riders at top speed. On a 250m track, these maneuvers will take place every second

Robert George

Successful modern six-day races have been held in Montreal and Toronto. Shown here are two riders in their rest cabin during a 1973 six-day event in Montreal.

lap (the fast men doing two laps, the slow ones doing one). Thus there will have been four changes before the teams prepare themselves for the first sprint for points. Points awarded will be three-two-one for the first three across the line every 10th lap. There will be a total of 20 sprints in this race, with double points on the last lap.

Each team tries to work the changes so that the faster of the two men contests the sprints — although this is not of vital importance. The ideal combination for a Madison team is to have a sprinter-type matched with a pursuit-type rider. This is how teams A and B are composed. Teams C and D consist of two individually strong riders, track all-rounders who also perform well in criteriums; team E has speed in the sprints, but lacks stamina; and team F lacks experience.

The first sprint is a closely fought affair between teams A, B and E, all of them wanting the psychological advantage of an early success. The verdict goes to B for three points, with E taking two points and A one. However, tracking the three leaders in the sprint was one of the strong C riders, who now puts in a sudden attack before the sprinters have a chance to relay with their partners. A gap of 100m, almost half a lap, is quickly opened before team C makes its change. The change is made after the second man swoops down the banking so he will be at top speed when he takes over the pace.

The move by team C is typical in a Madison. Team C is now in the same straight as the pack and closing before an effective chase can be organized. The attacking rider soon catches the team F man who had been dropped in the sprint, and then latches onto the front group to give C its one lap lead. This would be the position on the scoreboard:

1.	Team C		0 pts
2.	Team B	at 1 lap	3 pts
3.	Team E	"	2 pts
4.	Team A	"	1 pt
5.	Team D	"	0 pts
6.	Team F	"	0 pts

Besides gaining laps, as C has just done, it is also possible to lose laps. During long "jams" — periods of concerted attacking with several teams involved and gaining on the pack — weaker teams often get dropped. If this had happened to team F, and they had been caught by the pack, they would be "at 2 laps" instead of "at 1 lap."

The most spectacular, and exciting, Madisons are those in which several teams are equally strong. If they are good in the chases and in the sprints, laps are hard to gain and points are vital. Such a situation could develop in our example, and the positions after 45 kms (20 laps to go) could read:

1.	Team B	27 pts
2.	Team A	20 pts
3.	Team C	15 pts

4.	Team E	at 2 laps	30 pts
5.	Team D	at 5 laps	10 pts
6.	Team F	at 10 laps	6 pts

Team E has proved best in the sprints, but has dropped two laps behind the three leaders, with B leading A by seven points. With two more sprints to come (double points on the final lap, remember), there is a maximum tally of nine points available for team A if they want to finish overall winners on points. This would be a long shot. Therefore, teams A and C will attempt to gain a clear lap on B in this final period of the race.

Team C attacks first, gaining 50m, but they're held to this limit by B's powerful riding at the front of the string. Team C is reeled in just before the penultimate sprint, so team A immediately counterattacks to take the three points. Teams C and E come past the tiring B team, which means only four points separate the two leaders, with six points available in the last sprint.

The pack re-forms after the sprint. Teams A and C must quickly decide if they are to attack and gain the lap they need for outright victory, or play a waiting game and hope that B is not placed in the sprint. In reality, particularly in pro racing, money would probably be promised to team C by either A or B to help them win (with C accepting the best offer.) But this is a theoretical race, and we will assume that there are no such coalitions.

By chance, A and C attack at the same time, swapping pace as they draw away from the pack. The move breaks up the field, leaving riders spaced all round the track: A and C at the front and gaining, E and F at the back, losing ground, while B and D are in-between. In such a situation it is often difficult to determine who is in the pack, or when a team has gained a lap. This is why it is essential to have experienced officials to make the necessary decisions, and to record the current lap and points position of every team.

In our race, B and D constitute the pack, and it is up to A or C to catch them if they want to win. The final kilometer (four laps left) is reached with the pair still 100m short of their target. Team A has decided to let its pursuer put in a final burst of three laps (instead of the usual two) and to hand over to the team's sprinter with only 1½ laps remaining. The plan works perfectly, with team C being dropped in the process. A's sprinter only has to make up 25m when he takes over. Sprinting flat out, he goes by B and D on the final bend to make the final result:

1.	Team A		29 pts
2.	Team B	at 1 lap	29 pts
3.	Team C	"	21 pts

That, therefore, is Madison racing: a tough, exciting event that brings out the best of a rider's ability, skill and tactical sense. It is also one of the most physically demanding of track events — almost a non-stop session of sprint intervals lasting for one or two hours, perhaps longer if it is over the 100 km distance. Each rider has to be alert to tactical moves, and he must have a perfect understanding with his partner to be in the correct position for each change. It is an event which demands many of the attributes of a roadman, allied with the skills and dexterity of a trackman.

A leading example of a team that excels in Madison racing is the duo of Patrick Sercu, former world sprint champion who is now a top roadman, and Eddy Merckx, who has competed on the track since his novice days. This pair is not seen competing together very much in six-day races these days, but they are almost unbeatable when they do team up.

Anyone who has seen Sercu competing in a six-day can testify to the electrifying burst of speed he still possesses despite his long road mileages. His speed is good enough for him to feel confident in taking any vital sprint he wants during the course of a Madison. His confidence is further enhanced by his brilliant positional sense and superb timing.

Showmanship is one of the main characteristics of a top six-day star, and Sercu's swift, swooping sprints, when he comes from, say, 20 lengths back to take a tire-width's decision,

Robert George

In relaying a teammate into the race, a six-day racer will use what is called a "Madison sling." This is executed in the fashion shown above or by grabbing a pad fitted into a narrow pocket on the other man's hip and throwing him into the action.

endear him to the crowds far more than if he won from the front by a wider margin.

Merckx's forte is his strength in a long "jam". The sustained pressure and speed he can display can be just as thrilling as a

101

tightly fought sprint. He also has a fine sprint himself, which gives the Merckx-Sercu combination a double cutting edge.

Another hallmark of a six-day master is his ability to perform well with whatever rider he is paired. (It is a favorite ploy of promoters to team up a man such as Sercu with a top local name who will help to draw more spectators.) Some of the top riders of the past who had this ability include Holland's Peter Post, who holds the world record for the number of six-day wins; Belgium's Rik Van Steenbergen, a multi world road champion and classic winner; and the pre-war star "Torchy" Peden of Canada, who achieved the majority of his victories on North American soil, when six-day racing was still big on this continent.

Post dominated six-day racing more than perhaps any man has done in the past, or is likely to do in the future. Such was his influence with the other riders in the six-day "circus" that he would carry the responsibility of a whole race on his own broad shoulders, dictating the pattern, and often the results, of each event.

His particular specialty was racing behind dernys – the finely adjusted, motorized bicycles which are capable of a maximum speed of around 45 mph and are directly controlled by the pedaling rate of the pacer. (Derny-paced events are a highlight of most European "sixes," a typical formula being a race in which the first half is ridden by the lesser names, with the big stars being relayed in for the final section.)

When Post came into a race, it was arranged that his partner would have lost, say, two laps on the leaders. This meant Post would have to race flat out to get back on level terms, let alone have a chance of winning.

This is what the crowds paid to see. The roar of the derny engines working at their maximum and the spectacle of a cyclist lapping a 200m bowl at over 40 mph is an irresistable combination.

Behind the buzzing derny, Post was the master of timing, just as Sercu is in a sprint. He would leave himself about a half-lap margin to make up in the final few laps and then seem to go into overdrive, shouting and gesticulating at his pacer to go faster. The spectators would be on their feet as the gap melted before their eyes. The "Flying Dutchman" would zoom past the astounded leader in the final meters to clinch the narrowest of victories.

Six-day races are not all pure spectacle, and the quality of racing in a Madison can be as high as in any road classic or Olympic pursuit match. Madison racing also demands as much, or even more, tactical knowledge as any other track event. On paper, two men can appear to be an unbeatable team. But without experience and expert knowledge of tactics they can be made to look the rawest of novices by hardened professionals. This was proved perhaps better than ever when Merckx and Sercu first appeared as a team in the professional ranks.

At the time, Merckx was reigning world amateur road champion and Sercu had won the kilometer time trial in the Tokyo Olympics. They had every intention of showing the professionals, and the bike fans, just how good they were. On physical ability, the two young Belgians were probably better than most of the professionals, but Post was then in his prime and the six-day riders were part of a very exclusive club. Their livelihood depended upon their successful reputations being maintained. A new twosome, whatever their names, would have to prove themselves before they could be accepted into this "high society."

Merckx-Sercu started out as they predicted, but their early successful attacks did not continue for long. The crunch came when, immediately after gaining a lap, Merckx-Sercu attacked again. This was too much for Post and his henchmen, and when the two upstarts had moved half-a-lap clear the order was given to leave them there. Every time that Merckx or Sercu tried to accelerate, the other teams (riding in unison) would instantly accelerate to match their speed to that of the Belgians.

Laps passed, minutes ticked by, and still Merckx-Sercu remained that tantalizing half-lap ahead. They were too proud to give in and admit that they couldn't take another lap, which played right into the hands of their opponents. Eventually, after the newcomers had ridden themselves to the point of exhaustion, the pack swooped.

Merckx and Sercu were too tired to respond to the increased tempo, losing lap after lap to the established stars. They had learned a very harsh lesson; whenever the chips are down in Madison racing, brains will always defeat brawn.

In regular Madison racing, the knowledge of tactics is perhaps less important than the acquisition of basic skills — vigilance, changing technique and timing. It is vital to know when to attack, when to chase and when to defend. These skills can only be gained from competition. For a novice rider to learn the tricks of the trade first-hand, it is advisable for him to team up with a seasoned Madison rider. It is possible to practice Madison changes in training, for instance, but it is a far different problem to change smoothly in a fast, weaving bunch of riders in the actual competition.

As for basic fitness training, there is little difference between training for Madison racing and for any other distance event on the track. Given a broad base of road miles to build on, the best way to acquire speed is to compete in as many track meets as possible. Do not be afraid to attack in 10-mile races — you will be increasing your resistance at racing speeds. And get as much sprinting practice as possible in the elimination and points races.

Another way to increase your endurance, and retain speed, is to train "behind the motors," such as the derny. Interval training will also be of great benefit, as this type of effort is very similar to actual Madison racing. On an outdoor track, these intervals could be one lap fast, one lap slow, one lap fast. Use half-lap intervals if the track is very big.

This year, for the first time in many years, the US will have a national Madison championship. Of course, such events are common in Europe. There is also a European Professional Madison title contested during the winter on an indoor velodrome. The attraction of such a championship is that both roadmen and trackmen can compete on almost equal terms, giving rise to competitive, exciting racing.

With more tracks, and more riders competing on them,

Madison racing could well see a revival in America. If that happens, then perhaps the American sports fan will again come to appreciate just how spectacular a six-day race can be.

FIVE

Building A Velodrome
by James C. McCullagh

The new Trexlertown (Penn.) velodrome is rated as probably the best in the US. James C. McCullagh has been involved with this facility since the planning stages. Although James has done a lot of road racing, he considers himself mainly a journalist. An associate editor with Rodale Press in Emmaus, Penn., he's written for almost all the cycling publications in the US. He's also the author of the book, American Bicycle Racing, *which will be published this fall.*

Just before the April, 1976 opening of the Trexlertown velodrome, I asked one of the riders what he thought about the new facility. "Great," he responded, "but it's really just a beginning. We need tracks in every state, every city. Look at the Russians. In Moscow alone there are about a dozen tracks. That's what we need."

The potential of American track riders, as revealed in recent international competition, is startling. Although the US has but a dozen tracks of varying quality, our track riders have done exceedingly well. The accomplishments of Sue Novara and Sheila Young have seized the imaginations of Europeans and Americans, as have the performances of Mary-Jane Reoch, a silver medalist in the individual pursuit at the 1975 World Championships.

Similarly, American track men have accomplished mighty things in recent years. Surely, the showing of the 1975 Pan-

American track team under the guidance of Jack Simes can be considered the high point of American men's racing. Steve Woznick was superb in winning the sprint gold medal at Mexico City. Equally memorable was the performance of the victorious team pursuit. Paul Deem, Roger Young, Ron Skarin and Ralph Therrio rode, in the vernacular, like West Germans, and swept past politics and impossible odds to take the prize.

The accomplishments of Mexico City were not lost on the United States Olympic Committee, which called for Federal monies for the construction of more velodromes. Simultaneously, there appears to be a grass roots movement in the country with the aim of doubling the number of velodromes within a matter of years.

At present, there are tracks in San Diego, San Jose and Encino, Calif.; Alpenrose, Ore.; Redmond, Wash.; Milwaukee, Wis.; Northbrook, Ill.; Detroit, Mich.; St. Louis, Mo.; East Point, Ga.; Trexlertown, Penn., and Flushing, N.Y.

Tracks are being considered, planned or constructed in the following areas: Marin County, Santa Barbara, Claremont and Orange County in California; Miami and Homestead in Florida; Louisville, Ky.; Warren, Mich.; Edina, Minn.; Albuquerque, N.M.; Dayton, Ohio; Jackson, Miss.; Rocky Mount, N.C.; Annston, Ala.; and Camden, S.C.

There are also several velodromes in Canada: Toronto, Winnipeg, Vancouver, Calgary and Montreal. Edmonton, Alberta, has started construction on a velodrome for the 1978 Commonwealth Games.

It is not unreasonable to suppose that within two or three years America could have 30 or more velodromes. Interestingly, Jack Simes, '76 US Olympic track coach, has remarked that Europe is looking to the US to bring back track racing. "Since track racing is falling off in Europe," says Simes, "they see America as the place to bring back the glamor of track racing which has been lost to the road. They also see that we are producing some very good track riders."

Plenty of reasons suggest the advisability, and perhaps inevitability, of more velodromes in the US: a desire on the

Aerial view of the Trexlertown velodrome site early in the construction phase.

part of thousands of cyclists to have adequate facilities for racing and training; a desire on the part of millions of Americans to have a safe place, away from automobile traffic, to ride for pleasure and health; and a desire on the part of communities to utilize a velodrome as a center of safety instruction. Also, it is predicted that there will be more bikes than cars on the road by 1980, so there is an increased interest on the part of the government and private sector in being ready to meet the demands of the future.

In truth, the US appears to be entering her second velodrome phase. Unlike many sports which are only now enjoying their heyday, bike racing, particularly on the track, caught the popular imagination between 1890-1920. That was the Golden Age of track racing; reliable estimates indicate that more than 100 velodromes dotted 'the US during those years.

However, the invention of the internal combustion engine lured men away from bicycles. Before long outdoor velodromes gave way to motorcycle tracks or were moved indoors. By 1930, outdoor track racing had all but ceased in the US. Fortunately for the sport, outdoor velodrome construction

The velodrome banking being compacted with a back hoe.

experienced a rebirth in the 1960s thanks to the industry and commitment of people such as Frank Brilando, H. M. Huffman, Jr., Keith Kingbay and others. Due in part to their efforts, tracks were constructed in Milwaukee, Northbrook, Flushing and Encino.

PRESENT TRACK SITUATION

From the early days of track revival in this country, attention has been given to tracks which can serve the full gamut of a community's needs. Using an argument that is still valid today, Frank Brilando noted more than 10 years ago that for all-around cycling, a "track of four or five laps to the mile is a very good size. Inexperienced riders and youngsters on stock bikes can easily ride a track in this size range."

Not surprisingly, Brilando's plans for one-fourth and one-fifth mile tracks have served a valuable need. The most recent track built along those lines is the one at East Point, Ga. Nonetheless, much of the information in these plans has been superceded by the "Rome" velodrome plans, translated from the Italian by California engineer E. C. Steffani, at the request of Robert Tetzlaff of the USCF. These plans for 333.3- and

Rodale Press

Initial build-up of the track banking. The Trexlertown velodrome was built according to the "Rome" plans, which allow for a smooth, fast track with excellent banking and transitions. The "Rome" plans are not only ones which satisfy Union Cycliste Internationale *requirements but they are the most in demand.*

110

Delivering crushed-stone sub-base to the track site. Note that the wide access road allows convenient access to the track.

400-meter velodromes come at a propitious time. And if there is a discernible trend in the US regarding velodrome construction, it appears to be in the direction of such metric velodromes which satisfy *Union Cycliste Internationale* requirements and a community's needs. (Plans can be obtained through the USCF.)

As important as the half-dozen tracks of the 1960s were in the promotion of racing at the grass roots level, the general impression is that, from a structural and engineering point of view, the design of these early velodromes could be improved — and, in fact, had to be improved in future if the US was to challenge at the Olympic level. Some of the rider criticisms of these tracks were: curve banking inadequate; straights too steep; transition inadequate; straights too short; and surface too bumpy.

According to Steffani, most of the deficiencies of these tracks could be avoided through attention to proper design features. "Criticisms of inadequate banking, short straights and rapid transition," he writes, "can be avoided by more careful selection of geometry. Bumpiness is a result of either settle-

111

ment, consolidation due to faulty construction, or difficulties experienced in paving."

Steffani's translated "Rome" plans require that a bicycle track design answer three conditions:

1) To permit or allow the racer a mild entry into the curve with an easy or mild connection;

2) To permit or allow the racer an easy exit from the curve by means of a connection that will permit him to arrive at the straight without swerving, jolting or dispersion of any kind, bearing in mind that at the exit of the curve and on the straight the athlete develops the maximum finishing effort; and

3) The track has a banking of the straight in order to reduce to the minimum the jolting or swerving, so that the racers can produce the maximum effort or force that concludes each race.

"In other words," Steffani continues, "a bicycle track is a curved course where you can ride at top speed. The track must have a smooth surface. The banking, or superelevation, must be designed to allow the rider to negotiate the corners without sliding or striking a pedal. The entrance or exits to and from the banked corners must have approach transitions sufficient to take the rider from the steeper to flatter banking without excessive side motion."

Since the UCI has established certain criteria for the design and construction of tracks subsequent to January, 1973 if the track is to be approved for UCI competition or World Championships, the Steffani translation appears to have filled a design gap in track construction — at least in North America. While these are not the only plans which satisfy UCI requirements, they are most in demand and have been tested in diverse climatic locations in the country.

In the short history of the Trexlertown velodrome, it has been our experience that these plans allow for a smooth, fast track with excellent banking and transitions. Jack Simes, Olympic track coach and velodrome director, has said that Trexlertown is as close to a perfect track as has been built in the US. The best track riders in the country have ridden the Trexlertown velodrome and confirm Simes' assessment.

Nonetheless, we do not wish to propose this track as a prototype for the country. Every area is unique and will require special consideration. All the following items, which vary from region to region, must be taken into consideration by any group or community planning to build a velodrome: land costs, construction, engineering and architectural costs, topography, environmental impact, freeze-thaw cycle, rainfall, local soil types, sub-base requirements, private/public involvement, etc.

On the other hand, since the Trexlertown velodrome was so carefully planned, with each construction stage recorded and photographed, we feel our effort has much to offer interested parties.

FUNDING SOURCES

As so many areas of the country have discovered, financing a velodrome is a costly undertaking.

Technical Bulletin, Number Three, published by the Bureau of Outdoor Recreation (July, 1975), provides the following information concerning funding sources:

"Funding for velodrome development can come from several potential sources. These include: private sources, local funds, Federal sources, or a combination of two or more of these.

"Private sources generally include contributions from private citizens. These contributions may, of course, range from numerous small individual gifts to a complete private financing of the project by a single contributor.

"Surprisingly, the more common method of private involvement with the existing velodromes has been the large contribution. This is not to say that a determined group might not be able to raise the necessary capital by cake and cookie sales. But there is a strong likelihood that local civic organizations and even private enterprises might well be interested in making suitable contributions. Of course, since the local situation will be entirely different for each locality, the only real advice that can be given is to leave no stone unturned.

"Local public funds are made available by a city, county or state. In general, these funds take two major forms: general

A workman hand-troweling poured concrete to provide the best possible finish. A steel-trowel finish is recommended over a broom finish for safety reasons.

funds and special funds. General funds are a part of the general budget and could be voted for velodrome development purposes by the local government...Special funds are created by bond issues and other revenue raising devices and devoted to a particular purpose. Often a local political jurisdiction will create a bond issue for a general specific purpose, such as recreation, thereby giving an opportunity for inclusion of velodrome funds as part of the whole bond issue.

"In some cases it may be possible to utilize Federal funding sources. Generally, these sources will require that proof be furnished that the resulting project will be of benefit to the general public...

"A source of Federal assistance is the Land and Water Conservation Fund (L&WCF) administered by the Bureau of Outdoor Recreation through a system of State-appointed liaison officers... If a velodrome project is approved, the Fund can pay up to 50 per cent of the costs. Local share can be 'in kind,' that is, in the form of such elements as labor, materials and land.

Test concrete slab shown in the foreground. Note the simple forms and stone base, also the "compacted" track in background ready for the stone sub-base.

The velodrome at East Point, Ga., is one of the few velodrome projects which has received L&WCF assistance.

"Other Federal programs that may offer potential for assistance are the Community Development funds administered by the Department of Housing and Urban Development, the Environmental Protection Agency's recreation grant program, and possibly even the facilities' improvement programs of such agencies as the National Park Service and the Corps of Engineers."

Clearly, there is no one avenue to obtaining velodrome funds.

PRELIMINARY CONSTRUCTION CONSIDERATIONS

To cut costs, vigorous attempts should be made to achieve a donation of land for the velodrome project. A community should also be on the lookout for natural oval or bowl-shaped areas suitable for track construction. The builders of the East Point velodrome saved considerable excavation costs because of the "natural" velodrome site. The proposed Wright Brothers

115

velodrome in Dayton, Ohio, will also be built in a natural bowl.

When a site has been determined, a thorough topographic survey should be made, and a soil sampling and analysis conducted. A rainfall study should cover the maximum storms that could occur every one, five, 10 and 25 years. These steps will determine drainage costs.

Drainage costs at Trexlertown were approximately $30,000, although the original estimates were far less. Since proper drainage affects the stability, smoothness and transitions of the track, this feature should be given careful attention. In this vein, we took pains to use crushed stone wherever practical around the track to reduce water run-off associated with asphaltic surfaces. Accordingly, adjacent parking lots should be surfaced with a modified crushed-stone. While our drainage costs were relatively high, we consider the expense well justified. Minutes after exceedingly heavy spring rains, the track and surrounding areas have dried.

Necessary preliminary work in building a velodrome should include an environmental impact study. A crucial part of the study would be an analysis of changes in traffic pattern and flow. Don't underestimate the drawing potential of your velodrome. At Trexlertown we postulated parking requirements on an expected crowd of 1,000 spectators. However, by the third week of the season we were drawing over 3,000 fans, which required parking space for over 1,000 cars. Fortunately, a nearby parking lot could be utilized.

GRADING AND BANKING

Most velodrome sites require that topsoil be stripped, drainage facilities put in, and the banking built up to an appropriate slope. Steffani writes: "Assuming the soil to be of a coarse granular nature with little likelihood of expansiveness, and the shrinkage of compaction to be approximately 30 per cent, cutting the infield to a depth of 3¼ feet should yield approximately 15,000 cubic yards, which when compacted would provide the approximate 10,500 yards needed to construct the upper 8¼ feet of fill and replace the volume displaced by compaction preparatory to the placement of fill."

In other words, if your velodrome site is generally level and made up of coarse, granular soil, the soil at the site should be sufficient to satisfy your banking requirements. If not, "import" the soil and regrade surrounding area to get sufficient fill for the banking.

This is a relatively simple job, requiring less than two months of work. It should be noted that the available construction equipment can bring the soil to the necessary compaction without allowing six months or so for possible settling.

TRACK SURFACE

Most authorities recognize that a board track is the ultimate surface for riding and it is good news that such a track is being constructed in Edina, Minn. Board tracks, though ideally suited for indoor velodromes, are not necessarily suited for outdoor facilities, however. As Frank Brilando has noted, "It is not practical to paint a board track as the least dampness will make the surface slippery. The main disadvantages to the outdoor board track are short surface life (about eight years in most climates) and, generally, (using boards is) an expensive method of construction on a large track. Therefore, multi-purpose outdoor velodromes, for obvious reasons, appear to be what the country is interested in."

Some of the best-known velodromes in the US, including Kenosha, Encino and Northbrook, initially had track surfaces of clay construction, treated with oil or plastic material. Later, permanent surfaces were added. This might well be a desirable option for some communities.

Most of the operating velodromes have asphalt surfaces. Two recently constructed tracks, East Point and Marymoor, Wash., have surfaces of reinforced and non-reinforced concrete respectively. East Point used 3000-point standard dry concrete mix for the straightaways. For the turns and steep banking, they fashioned an aggregate mix. The track was laid in 18-foot lengths with the use of forms. The desired finish was obtained through the laborious process of grinding the concrete.

Rodale Press

A crew of workmen paving and finishing one of the steepest sections of the track. A cement called Chem Comp was used. Finishers had little difficulty working the mix, even on steep bankings. Note the "final" smooth surface on the right.

The track apron was laid first, so there would be a bottom form for the rest of the work. The apron was "broken" at regular intervals to allow for freezing.

The Marymoor track used standard Portland cement, with saw-cuts filled with an elastic sealant, every 12½ feet. The surface was given a "broom" finish.

Since the types of cement used at East Point and Marymoor did not provide the most desirable finish, we considered other options, including asphalt, when building the Trexlertown velodrome. However, in the opinion of Steffani, "Asphaltic... surfaces are to be avoided — the difficulty of laying hot asphalt on a steep banking and the requirements for hand rolling has been the first cause for our bumpy tracks at New York and San Jose."

If at all possible, we wanted to avoid frequent joints and saw-cuts which occasionally contribute to bumpiness. Similarly, we sought the smoothest possible finish. We also desired a surface which wouldn't negate the beautiful transitions allowed for in the "Rome" velodrome plans, and would withstand the severity of our northern winter.

Fortunately, we discovered that a "new" cement called Chem Comp, developed about seven years ago, can be put down in very large sections without saw-cuts. After a test-slab was successfully laid on the first turn, the engineers decided that this cement answered our needs. Within a month, twelve 90-foot sections of Chem Comp were poured. Crushed rock was used as a base and steel mesh as a reinforcement. Expansion joints were located between slabs.

Contrary to what we expected, the finishers had little difficulty working the mix, even on the steep banking. Working from a type of "ladder," which allowed good mobility, a team of up to a dozen finishers provided a steel-trowel finish. A steel-trowel finish is definitely recommended over a broom finish, which can present a real hazard to the rider. Accordingly, while there have been spills at Trexlertown, no serious abrasions have been reported.

Based on engineering estimates, the Trexlertown surface has "passed the test" by holding up well during the winter. Although this type of surface might not be suitable for all regions, it will surely answer the needs of many.

PERIPHERAL CONSIDERATIONS

Part of the attractiveness of the "Rome" velodrome plans is that they allow for access around and into the velodrome. The eight-foot apron specified in the plans is ideally suited to velodrome traffic. And the 12-foot-wide access "road" above the track allows ample room for the movement of spectators.

The track railing, three feet high and of wood construction, provides safety for both riders and spectators.

Bleachers should not be placed too close to the track, impairing visibility and causing congestion. We made this mistake with our first set of bleachers at Trexlertown, situating them too close to the start-finish line and placing them too low, negating the visibility of spectators in the first few rows.

If at all possible, lights should be installed during the first

Rodale Press

Track completely poured except for one slab, which allowed access of heavy equipment to the infield. Track apron is stacked out and ready for blacktop. Stone is in place on the access road above the track.

construction phase, minimizing future disruption of the site and allowing a full schedule of night racing from the beginning. At Trexlertown we have found that eight light standards (creosote poles) with six 1500-watt lamps per pole provide even lighting around the entire track. We have left room on the light standards for the mounting of additional lamps if and when the need for night television coverage arises.

A chain-link fence was constructed around the velodrome to ensure spectator control and the collection of admission charges.

SITE AND CONSTRUCTION COSTS

Constructing a velodrome which meets UCI requirements is a costly undertaking. In his *Design and Construction of Bicycle Tracks*, Steffani estimates that topsoil work, drainage, banking, access road at the top of the track, surface, fencing and gates would cost up to $78,000. Below are some of the representative costs for the construction of the Trexlertown velodrome:

The completed track. Trexlertown has been described as being as close to a perfect track as has been built in the US. Total cost of the facility—including land cost—came to almost $500,000.

1) Land Cost. Although the land was donated, it is estimated that the five acres are valued at $5,000 an acre — $25,000.

(*Note:* Land values vary greatly. The City of Dayton estimates that the five acres it donated to the Wright Brothers Velodrome project is valued at $90,000. High land costs are just another reason for a community to try to acquire velodrome land through donation.)

2) Original contract for topsoil stripping, preliminary grading, buildup of banking, compaction of soil, drainage, engineering and architectural costs, miscellaneous expenditures — $88,000.

3) General contractor for general requirements, sitework, underslab drainage, bituminous and stone paving, fences and gates, seeding (on the banking and infield), concrete paving, miscellaneous concrete, steel reinforcement, masonry, miscellaneous metals, bleachers (capacity 1200), special finish, railing and gates, well-house for pump and electrical equipment — $238,000.

121

4) Electrical contractor for permits and inspections, excavation, galvinized conduit and fitting, PVC conduit underground, transformer, safety switch, unit heater, lighting poles, lighting fixtures, lamps — $67,000.

5) Shower, toilet facilities and locker rooms — $45,000.

The total is $463,000. This figure doesn't include engineering and architectural fees, which generally come to about 10 per cent of the final construction cost.

It should be noted that while the above figures will vary from region to region, we feel they are representative. The City of Dayton, which is planning to build a similar track in the near future, projects similar site and construction costs. That does not mean, however, that communities cannot build tracks for less. The East Point track seems to have cost less but that facility still doesn't have lights or changing rooms.

For all practical purposes, the Trexlertown velodrome is a "finished" track, with plans to expand locker room and bleacher capacities in the future. In the early weeks of the 1976 season the track has been drawing Friday night crowds of well over 3,000 in a community which months ago did not know what a velodrome was.

The point is that while the initial financial outlay for a velodrome might be high, the track can quickly become revenue-producing. The people behind the Wright Brothers Velodrome in Dayton, Ohio have estimated that a National Championship in their area would generate $200,000 for the community.

All in all, we feel that we have done most things right in the construction of the Trexlertown velodrome. No account can accurately describe the many thousands of hours the architects, engineers and construction crews devoted to the project. Should your community decide to build a velodrome, you might like to visit our track and talk with those involved in its construction. We would be happy to arrange a meeting.

Appendix: Velodromes in North America

UNITED STATES

- Alpenrose, Ore., near Portland—Alpenrose Velodrome. Concrete surface, 41-degree maximum banking—steepest in the US, 1/6 mile. Built in 1955 and re-built in 1967. Contact D. Curey, 5445 S.W. Childs Road, Lake Grove, Ore. 97034.

- Detroit, Mich.—Dorais Velodrome. Cement, 28-degree banking, 1/5 mile. Built in '69. Contact Fred Cappy, 25897 Chippendale, Apt. A, Roseville, Mich. 48066.

- East Point, Ga.—Dick Lane Velodrome. Concrete, 33-degree banking, 1/5 mile. Opened in '75. Contact East Point Track Association, c/o Ken Reed, 4545 Chaldwell Lane, Dunwoody, Ga. 30338.

- Encino, Calif.—Encino Velodrome. Cement, 34-degree banking, 250m. Opened in '61. Contact Joe Yoder, (213) 785-9386.

- Kenosha, Wis. Fifth of a mile blacktop track located in Washington Park. Contact Theo Kron, 5843 Capri Lane, Morgan Grove, Ill. 60053.

- Kissena Park, N.Y.—Siegfried Stern Velodrome. Asphalt, 22-degree banking, 400m. Opened in '63. Contact Al Toefield, 87-66 256th St., Floral Park, N.Y. 11001.

- Milwaukee, Wis.—Brown Deer Track. Asphalt, 23-degree banking, 400m. Built in '48 for the Olympic trials. Contact the Milwaukee Wheelmen, c/o 13685 West Graham, New Berlin, Wis. 53151.

- Northbrook, Ill. Paved track, 400m in length, with a maximum 18-degree banking. Frequent site of the US Nationals. Contact Northbrook Cycling Committee, c/o 1954 Thornwood, Northbrook, Ill. 60062.

- Redmond, Wash.—Marymoor Velodrome. Cement, 28-degree banking, 400m. Opened in '75. Contact Jim Stillmaker, Director, 2417 South Orcas St., Seattle, Wash. 98108.

- San Jose, Calif.—Santa Clara County Velodrome. Asphalt, 25-degree banking, 333.3m. Opened in '63. Contact Jim Gentes, 10421 Corte de Madrid, Cupertino, Calif. 95014.

- St. Louis, Mo.—Penrose Velodrome. Asphalt, 23-degree banking, 1/5 mile. Opened in the early '60s. Contact Chester Nelson Sr., 4701 Natural Bridge, St. Louis, Mo. 63115.

- Trexlertown, Pa.—Trexlertown Velodrome. Cement, 27-degree banking, 333.3m. Opened in '75. Contact Jack Simes, Rodale Press, 33 E. Minor St., Emmaus, Pa. 18049.

CANADA

- Calgary, Alta.—Glenmore Velodrome. Asphalt, 30-degree banking, 400m. Completed in '75, just in time for the Canadian National Championships. Contact Chris Wood, 731 Archwood Road S.E., Calgary, Alta. T2J 1C1.

- Montreal, Quebec—'76 Olympic Velodrome. Wood, 285m, completed in '76. Contact Maurice Jeffries, Cycling Coordinator, COJO '76, Box 1976, Montreal, Que. H3C 3A6.

- Vancouver, B.C. A handsome 246m hemlock track located in China Creek Park. Opened in '72, 45-degree banking. Contact Vancouver C-Trac Society, Box 34156, Vancouver, B.C.

- Winnipeg, Man.—Winnipeg Velodrome. Concrete, 45 degrees, 254m. Built in '67 for the Pan-American Games. Contact Erick M. Oland, 2 Mt. Royal Crescent, Winnipeg, Man.

- Woodbridge, Ont., near Toronto—The International Velodrome. Concrete, 254.8m, 45-degree max banking. Built in '76. Contact Dave Viney, 54-25th St., Toronto, Ont.

PROPOSED TRACKS IN THE US AND CANADA

- Albuquerque, N. M. Contact Gary Diggs, 800 Alvarado S.E., Albuquerque, N. M. 87108.

- Dayton, O.—Wright Brothers Velodrome. Contact Dayton Cycling Club.

- Edina, Minn. Contact Cecil Behringer, 4202 Mavelle Drive, Edina, Minn. 55435.

- Edmonton, Alta. (This 333.3m concrete track is being built for the '78 Commonwealth Games.) Contact Rudi Frahm, 14712-59A Street, Edmonton, Alta. T5A 1Y9.

- Louisville, Ky. Contact Louisville Velodrome Committee, 1737 Bardstown Road, Louisville, Ky. 40205.

- Marin County, Calif. Contact Marin County Velodrome Association, Box 35, San Anselmo, Calif. 94960.

- Santa Barbara, Calif. Contact Santa Barbara Velodrome Committee, Box 30193, Santa Barbara, Calif. 93105.

- San Diego, Calif. (The 333m Balboa Park Velodrome was scheduled to open at the end of June '76.) Contact Jerry Rimoldi, 5779 Theta Place, San Diego, Calif. 92120.

- Warren, Mich. Contact Mike Walden at Madison Velodromes Ltd., 19286 Kelly Road, Detroit, Mich. 48225.

Notes

Notes